Meet Your Chinese Zodiac Animal

中国生肖文化解读系列

The YEAR of the TIGER

生肖虎

Compiled by Zhang Lizhang（张立章）

Translated by Yan Chuanhai（闫传海）

SinolinguA

华语教学出版社

First Edition 2019

ISBN 978-7-5138-1642-7

Published by Sinolingua Co., Ltd
24 Baiwanzhuang Road, Beijing 100037, China
Tel: (86) 10-68320585 68997826
Fax: (86) 10-68997826 68326333
http://www.sinolingua.com.cn
E-mail: hyjx@sinolingua.com.cn
Facebook: www.facebook.com/sinolingua
Printed by Beijing Xicheng Printing Co., Ltd

Printed in the People's Republic of China

鼠 牛 虎
兔 龍 蛇
馬 羊 猴
鷄 狗 猪

虎

Introduction

Dear friend, how much do you know about traditional Chinese culture?

Let's try a riddle to start: "There are 12 of them, each person claims but one of them; they can only be found in China. What are they?"

If you can figure it out, it shows that you know something about Chinese culture. In fact, former Japanese Prime Minister Kakuei Tanaka put this riddle to Chinese Premier Zhou Enlai during his visit to China in September 1972 to enliven their meeting. The key to the riddle is "the 12-year cycle of animals in the Chinese zodiac", or simply "the 12 zodiac animals".

The riddle was a piece of cake for Premier Zhou, as the 12 zodiac animals are familiar to everyone in China. But what is the Chinese zodiac?

In Chinese, it is called 生肖 (shēngxiào). 生 means "be born", while 肖 means "resemble". In the eyes of the ancient Chinese, human beings are part of nature. People born in different lunar years correspond to specific animals. A person's character resembles that of his or her animal. The 12 animals are the Rat, Ox, Tiger, Rabbit, Dragon, Snake, Horse, Goat, [1] Monkey, Rooster, Dog and Pig. People thus use them to number the years in a 12-year cycle.

The Chinese people often mark the beginning of a year with the Spring Festival, which is the most important festival in the country. It corresponds with one of the 12 zodiac animals, which will in turn become the auspicious image of the festival. Most New Year pictures, couplets, and greetings will feature the zodiac animal.

"In the Year of the Rat, you will have good luck; in the Year of the Ox, you will grow stronger; in the Year of the Tiger, you will behave more bravely; in the Year of the Rabbit, you will become smarter; in the Year of the Dragon, you will have a promising career; in the Year of the Snake, you will be safe and sound; in the Year of the Horse, you will live a brilliant life; in the Year of the Goat, you will enjoy prosperity; in the Year of the Monkey, you will get a promotion; in the Year of the Rooster, you will win a prize;

---

① The Chinese character 羊 (yáng) refers to both the goat and the sheep. Therefore, the eighth zodiac animal can be named goat or sheep. In this book, goat is used for the sake of convenience.

in the Year of the Dog, you will flourish; in the Year of the Pig, you will become more prominent." This is a Chinese New Year greeting related to the 12 zodiac animals used to wish everyone the best every year.

In China, there is a tradition associated with the Spring Festival that has been handed down for over a thousand years. When meeting with people during the festival, one should offer felicitations to others as often as possible. If instead you were to utter something ominous, it is said that this utterance will come true. In addition, Chinese people often use different felicitations in different years. If the year happens to be a year of a zodiac animal that has a noble status based on traditional Chinese culture, a good image, or a name that shares a similar pronunciation with words portending good fortune, they will use the zodiac animal name in their New Year greetings. These zodiac animals are the Ox, Tiger, Rabbit, Dragon, Horse, Goat, Monkey, and Rooster. As for the other zodiac animals, which are the Rat, Snake, Dog and Pig, they do not appear in New Year greetings. Tiger is one of Chinese people's favorite zodiac animals. It symbolizes bravery, authority and power based on traditional Chinese culture. If you were born in 2010, the Year of the Tiger, your zodiac animal will be the tiger, which will become the mascot and protector of your life. In the Year of the Tiger, therefore, during the Spring Festival Chinese people often greet each other with such good wishes as:

1. I wish you a happy and auspicious Year of the Tiger!

祝您虎年快乐，吉祥如意！

Zhù nín hǔnián kuàilè , jíxiáng-rúyì !

2. I wish you great fortune in the Year of the Tiger!

祝虎年行大运，发大财！

Zhù hǔnián xíng dà yùn, fā dà cái !

3. Wish you great progress in your career in the Year of the Tiger!

祝您虎年事业发展如虎添翼！

Zhù nín hǔnián shìyè fāzhǎn rúhǔ-tiānyì !

4. Good health to you! Be as robust as a tiger!

祝您身体健康，如龙似虎！

Zhù nín shēntǐ jiànkāng, rúlóng-sìhǔ !

5. All the best in the Year of the Tiger!

祝您虎年万事如意！

Zhù nín hǔnián wànshì-rúyì !

引　言

亲爱的朋友，您对中国传统文化是否了解？

请您先猜个谜语。谜面是：“共有十二个，每人占一个，东洋西洋都没有，请问是什么？”

如果你猜出了正确答案，说明你对中国文化有一定的了解。这个谜语是1972年9月日本前首相田中角荣先生访华时，为活跃气氛，给时任中国总理的周恩来先生猜的一个谜语，谜底就是“十二生肖”。

这个谜语当然没能难住周恩来总理，因为每个中国人都熟知12生肖。那么，什么是中国人的“生肖”呢？

“生肖”的“生”就是“出生”的意思，“肖”是“相似”的意思。也就是说，在中国古人的观念里，作为自然界的普通一员，不同时间出生的人，就会与某一种动物相对应，其性格也会与该动物特征相似。这些动物分别是鼠、牛、虎、兔、龙、蛇、马、羊、猴、鸡、狗、猪，共12种。中国人就用这12种动物来纪年，12年一个循环，周而复始。

中国人以自己的传统节日——春节为一年之始，每一年的春节都以当年对应的生肖动物为节日图腾。春节时张贴的年画、春联和新年祝福语都会以当年的生肖为主题。

“鼠年运来，牛年身壮，虎年勇猛，兔年机巧，龙年飞腾，蛇年安康，马年奔放，羊年开泰，猴年高升，鸡年中奖，狗年兴旺，猪年响当当！”这就是一句以 12 生肖为主题的新年祝福语，寓意是“年年你都会有好运气。”

中国人有一个流传千百年的文化传统，在春节前后，见人要多说吉利话。传说如果在这个佳节期

间说不吉利的话会应验成真。但是，不同生肖年度的春节，中国人常用的吉利话也有所不同：在中国文化传统中地位高、形象好或者谐音吉利的生肖动物就会直接出现在吉祥话中，比如牛、虎、兔、龙、马、羊、猴、鸡；另外一些生肖动物并不适宜出现在吉利话中，如鼠、蛇、狗、猪等。如前所述，虎是中国人最喜欢的生肖动物之一，在中国传统文化观念中，虎是勇敢、权威和力量的象征。假如一个人出生在2010年，这一年在中国历法中正是虎年，那么你的属相就是虎，虎就成为你一生的吉祥物和保护神。因此，在虎年春节，中国人见面会以虎年好运为主题说些吉利话。

1）（祝您）虎年快乐，吉祥如意！

2）祝虎年行大运，发大财！

3）祝您虎年事业发展如虎添翼！

4）祝您身体健康，如龙似虎！

5）祝您虎年万事如意！

Contents
目录

Chapter Three

Chapter Four

子
丑
寅
卯
辰
巳
午
未
申
酉
戌
亥

Chapter One

Zodiac Culture in Everyday Chinese Life

The long-cherished Chinese zodiac tradition has been passed down from generation to generation and has become deep-rooted in people's minds. It is widely recognized among the Chinese people that the 12 zodiac animal signs are closely linked with people's personalities, destinies, lives and careers. Just as British people might talk about the weather when they first meet, Chinese people often ask what zodiac animal a person is when they meet for the first time. This can be explained for the following reasons:

First, it is a good way to deduce the age of a person. Since it's not very polite to ask another person's age directly, their zodiac animal coupled with their appearance can help one deduce a person's age.

Second, it serves as an ice-breaker and makes people feel at ease. Asking about zodiac animals is considered a common communication skill by Chinese people. When two people find they share the same zodiac animal, they will have a natural

affinity and be eager to talk with each other.

Chinese people tend to group themselves according to their zodiac animal signs out of the belief that those with the same sign possess similar personalities and characteristics. Hence, they like discussing in which zodiac animal year a prominent figure was born in their spare time. They even consider it a great honor if they find that they happen to share the same zodiac sign with a renowned historical or contemporary figure, such as Genghis Khan (born in the Year of the Horse), founder of the

Mongol Empire; Zhuge Liang (born in the Year of the Rooster), a statesman during the period of the Three Kingdoms (220-280) and a paradigm of wisdom and good virtue; Li Shimin (born in the Year of the Goat), the co-founder of the Tang Dynasty (618-907), a golden age in Chinese history; Deng Xiaoping (born in the Year of the Dragon), the late Chinese leader regarded as the chief architect of China's reform and opening-up; and Xi Jinping (born in the Year of the Snake), the current Chinese President.

Third, it can help people extrapolate other people's personalities. According to zodiac animal culture, people born in the same zodiac animal year often share similar personality traits, luck for wealth, professional achievements and marriage patterns. Some Chinese people even get to know and choose their spouses, co-workers or business partners by talking about their zodiac animals. This topic seems simple, but it has rich connotations to the Chinese people.

If you are born in the Year of the Tiger, what kind of character, luck and marriage will you have according to the Chinese zodiac? Please read the following introduction and see if it is true for you.

十二生肖

Characteristics of "Tigers"

Chinese people tend to believe that people born in the Year of the Tiger are born leaders or managers. This is because they are typically as brave as a tiger. Though they may be cavalier with money, they tend to have a greater aptitude for earning it, as they have clear goals and are determined in their actions. However, many often get into financial difficulties because they are unaware of the importance of saving money.

In terms of personality, people born in the Year of the Tiger are passionate, courageous, and decisive. They are resolute and tenacious; once they have set a goal, they will stop at nothing until they achieve it. Such people are ambitious, adventurous, and confident, and are perseverant in the face of adversity. They cherish honesty and integrity, and never break their promises.

Men born in the Year of the Tiger are independent, proactive and tend to be strong leaders. Women born in the Year of the Tiger are expressive, carefree, fashionable and open-minded; they flawlessly combine their social and family lives.

But people born in the Year of the Tiger are also quite

十二生肖

rebellious. Their overconfidence can lead to a strong stubborn streak, making it difficult for them to communicate smoothly with others. They are known as loners. Such people are often in want of romance and tend to treat their family members in an arbitrary and despotic manner.

Marriages for "Tigers"

Matchmaking related to the Chinese zodiac is intriguing. If the zodiac animals of a couple are a good match, they will enjoy a loving relationship and a happy life; otherwise, their marriage may not be satisfactory. For instance, for a man born in the Year of the Tiger, his best match is a woman born in the year of the rabbit, horse or dog. But for a woman born in the Year of the Tiger, her best match is a man born in the year of the horse, dog or pig.

This notion has exerted great influence on people's attitudes towards marriage for nearly two thousand years. During the Qing Dynasty (1616-1911) and dynasties before that, marriages were arranged by parents, while people themselves had no freedom to choose their spouses. People often considered the match of zodiac animals as one of the important factors in determining a marriage. This resulted in a great number of

tragic marriages during the long period of feudalism in China. However, young people today no longer cling to matches based on zodiac animals when they choose their boyfriends or girlfriends. At any rate, this remains an indispensable topic for chitchat among Chinese people.

Eminent Figures Born in the Year of the Tiger

According to the Chinese zodiac, many eminent people in Chinese history were born in the Year of the Tiger. They often had a strong character and behaved like a king. They are extraordinarily talented and confident. All of them had outstanding achievements.

The First Emperor of the Qin Dynasty

Born in 259 BC, the first emperor of China.

Zhang Heng

Born in 78 AD, an astronomer in the Eastern Han Dynasty (25-220).

Li Shizhen

Born in 1518, the author of *Compendium of Materia Medica*, a renowned herbalist in the Ming Dynasty (1368-1644).

Dr. Sun Yat-sen

Born in 1866, founder of the Kuomintang (the Nationalist Party of China). He put an end to the Chinese feudal monarchy and became the first president of the Republic of China.

In other countries, a lot of outstanding people were also born in the Year of the Tiger. They include:

Marco Polo

Born in 1254, an Italian explorer and the author of *The Travels of Marco Polo*.

Louis XIV

Born in 1638, the third king of the French Bourbon Dynasty (1589-1848).

Ludwig van Beethoven

Born in 1770, known as the greatest German symphony composer.

Karl Marx

Born in 1818, founder of Marxism and the international communist movement.

Georg Wilhelm Friedrich Hegel

Born in 1770, a renowned German philosopher, a representative of classical idealism.

Romain Roland

Born in 1866, a well-known French thinker, writer, music critic, and social activist.

Thomas Hunt Morgan

Born in 1866, an American biologist and geneticist.

Dwight David Eisenhower

Born in 1890, Supreme Commander of the Allied Expeditionary Forces in Europe in World War II, the 34th US President from 1953 to 1961.

中国邮政CHINA
120分

中国邮政CHINA
120分

120分
中国邮政CHINA

120分
中国邮政CHINA

120分
中国邮政CHINA

120分
中国邮政CHINA

中国邮政CHINA
120分

中国邮政CHINA
120分

120分
中国邮政CHINA

中国邮政CHINA
120分

120分
中国邮政CHINA

中国邮政CHINA
120分

第一章 中国人生活中的生肖文化

生肖文化在中国历史悠久，世代相传，家喻户晓，早已深深根植于中国人的血液之中。它与每个中国人的性格、命运、生活和事业紧密联系在一起，并得到了中国人的普遍认同。直到今天，人们初次见面时，问询对方的生肖也是常事，如同英国人见面谈论天气一样普通。这主要有以下几方面的原因：

一是通过询问生肖来推测对方的实际年龄。因为直接询问对方的年龄不太礼貌，所以可以通过间接询问对方的生肖后，再根据外貌特征显示的年龄范围基本可以确定对方的实际年龄。

二是谈论生肖可迅速打破尴尬，拉近双方的心理距离。这也是中国人常见的一种见面沟通技巧，尤其是当生肖相同时，两个人就有了天然的亲近感，话题自然打开。

在工作、生活中，中国人会不自觉地按照同一个生肖划分出小群体，以显得亲近。闲暇时人们还喜欢聊聊中国某一著名人物的生肖，还会以与历史伟人或当代名人的生肖相同而沾沾自喜。

比如：蒙古帝国的缔造者成吉思汗属马；被中国人公认为智慧与品德典范的三国时期政治家诸葛亮属鸡；中国古代“大唐盛世”的开创者李世民属羊；被誉为当代“中国社会主义现代化建设和改革开放总设计师”的前国家领导人邓小平属龙；现任的中国国家领导人习近平属蛇；等等。

三是根据生肖来推测对方的性格类型及特点。中国人认为，相同生肖的人往往具有类似的性格、财运、事业成就和婚姻状况等。一些中国人就是在谈论生肖的过程中了解、选择自己的婚恋对象、同事搭档和创业伙伴的。这个看似简单的生肖话题，却被中国人赋予了如此丰富多样的内涵。

按照中国生肖文化的观念，属虎人有着特定的性格、运气和婚姻状况。如果你是属虎的，你可以对照一下自己，看看有哪些特点与你相契合。

一、属虎人的性格特点

中国人认为，虎年出生的人往往具有过人的气魄和胆识，适合做领导或管理者。属虎的人不太看重金钱，但因做事目标明确、行动坚定而有较好的经济来源。也有属虎人因缺乏储蓄意识而常常让自己陷入经济拮据的状态。

在性格方面，属虎的人热情、勇敢，做事大胆果断；性格刚毅顽强，凡事认定目标，不完成绝不罢休。属虎的人极具雄心壮志和冒险精神，往往是越挫越勇，自信心强。属虎的人讲究诚信，说到做到，绝不反悔。

属虎的男性往往独立性强，具有较强的行动力和领导力。属虎的女性表达能力较强，自由、时髦、开放，能够把社会生活和家庭生活完美结合起来。

另一方面，属虎的人颇具叛逆性，往往因过于自信而固执己见，难以与人很好地沟通，喜欢独来独往。属虎人往往缺乏浪漫情调，对待家人也有独断专行倾向。

二、属虎人的姻缘

在恋爱、婚姻观念方面，中国生肖匹配观念十分奇特：如果生肖匹配，夫妻二人就会感情深厚，婚姻幸福；否则，就会不如人意。比如：属虎的男人适宜寻求生肖为兔、马和狗的女人作为结婚对象；属虎的女人则适宜嫁给生肖为马、狗、猪的男人为妻。

这种传统的婚姻选择观念已经影响了中国人长达近两千年。在以前的封建王朝时代，婚姻双方当事人没有自由选择的权利，父母是儿女婚姻的绝对决定者，而男女双方的生肖是否匹配是能否结婚的重要依据之一。没有人知道，在中国漫长的封建时代里，非自由选择的婚姻模式到底酿成多少婚姻悲剧！当然，这些早已成为了历史，今天的年轻人不再执着于生肖相配的恋爱观，可生肖是否匹配仍旧是中国人茶余饭后津津乐道的谈资。

三、属虎的中外名人

按照中国人生肖纪年的算法，中国历史上虎年出生的杰出人物非常多。他们个性鲜明，多有王者之风，往往拥有常人不及的天赋，而且自信心强，常常可以取得非凡成就。

中国历史上第一位皇帝——秦始皇（公元前259年出生）；

中国东汉天文学家——张衡(公元78年出生);

明朝著名医药学家、《本草纲目》的作者——李时珍（1518年出生）；

中国国民党创始人、中国封建帝制终结者、中华民国首任大总统——孙中山（1866年出生）；

中国以外，虎年出生的各国各界杰出人物主要有：

意大利旅行家、《马可·波罗游记》的作者——马可·波罗（1254年出生）；

法国波旁王朝第三位君主——路易十四（1638年出生）；

德国交响曲作家——路德维希·凡·贝多芬（1770年出生）；

国际共产主义运动的奠基人、马克思学说创始人——卡尔·马克思（1818年出生）；

德国著名哲学家、古典唯心主义哲学的主要

代表人物——格奥尔格·威廉·弗里德里希·黑格尔（1770年出生）；

法国著名思想家、作家、音乐评论家和社会活动家——罗曼·罗兰（1866年出生）；

美国生物学家与遗传学家——托马斯·亨特·摩尔根（1866年出生）；

二战时期盟军统帅、美国第34任总统——德怀特·戴维·艾森豪威尔（1890年出生）。

Chapter Two

The Origin and Cultural Significance of the Chinese Zodiac Animals

Methods of Year Designation in Ancient China

The Chinese people invented their calendar in ancient times. During the Xia Dynasty (c.2070-1600 BC), a fairly precise calendar was created. This is why the traditional Chinese calendar was also called the Xia calendar. This Xia calendar, however, was used to designate months rather than years and served as a guide for agricultural production and sacrificial activities. In China, the practice of designating years began during the Western Zhou Dynasty (1046-771 BC). Three methods of year designation were later developed, designating years by emperors' reign titles, by Heavenly Stems and Earthly Branches, and by Chinese zodiac animals respectively.

Emperor Wudi of Han (140-88 BC)

I. Using the emperor's reign title to designate a year

This method of designating years dates back to the reign of Emperor Wudi (140-88 BC) of the Western Han Dynasty. From then on, an emperor could adopt several reign titles. For example, Emperor Wudi of Han adopted eleven titles. During the Ming and Qing dynasties, an emperor could only adopt one reign title. A new emperor had to designate a different title in the following year after he ascended to the throne and keep that title until he abdicated or died. This convention continued until 1912, when the last emperor of the Qing Dynasty, Puyi, abdicated (Puyi's reign title was Xuantong). The practice of using the emperor's reign title to designate a year ended with the abolition of China's feudal monarchy.

II. Using Heavenly Stems and Earthly Branches to designate a year

Ancient Chinese chose ten astronomical phenomena and gave them a collective name of Heavenly Stems, which are referred to as 甲 (jiǎ) , 乙 (yǐ) , 丙 (bǐng) , 丁 (dīng) , 戊 (wù) , 己 (jǐ) , 庚 (gēng) , 辛 (xīn) , 壬 (rén) and 癸 (guǐ) . They have also been used as serial numbers. People in ancient China also divided the orbit of Jupiter revolving around the sun into 12 parts and gave them a collective name Earthly Branches, which includes 子 (zǐ), 丑 (chǒu), 寅 (yín), 卯 (mǎo), 辰 (chén), 巳 (sì), 午 (wǔ), 未 (wèi), 申 (shēn), 酉 (yǒu), 戌 (xū) and 亥 (hài). The ten Heavenly Stems and 12 Earthly Branches form 60 pairs in total, thus this year designation method adopts 60 years as a cycle with

甲子 (jiǎzǐ) as the first and 癸亥 (guǐhài) the last.

III. Using the Chinese zodiac to designate a year

The Chinese adopted the zodiac year designation during the Han Dynasty (206 BC-AD 220) with 12 years as a cycle. It was a novel approach to use the 12 animals to mark each year, making it easier for people to remember every year. After this approach was adopted, everyone had their own zodiac animal based on the year in which they were born. This is the beginning of the rich and unique zodiac culture created by the Chinese people.

The Gregorian calendar has been adopted in China to officially designate the year since the founding of the People's Republic of China in 1949. But the method of using the Chinese zodiac for year designation is still popular among the Chinese people. For example, 2010 can be called a tiger year, and the next tiger year will be 2022.

Origin of the Chinese Zodiac Animals

Why did the Chinese ancestors choose the Rat, Ox, Tiger, Rabbit, Dragon, Snake, Horse, Goat, Monkey, Rooster, Dog and Pig to be on their zodiac? How did their sequence come about? There is a popular legend among the Chinese people that explains it.

Once upon a time, the immortal Great White Golden Star reported to the Jade Emperor (the supreme God in Chinese mythology who ruled all the immortals and spirits in heaven and on earth) that people on earth didn't have a method to calculate the year and month, thus he proposed a convenient year designation method be devised to make it easier for people to plant and harvest crops based on seasonal changes. His advice was welcomed by the emperor, who then appointed an official to be in charge of zodiac affairs and to organize a river-crossing contest for animals. The rules were that the 12 animals that crossed the river and reached the Heavenly Palace first would be granted titles as the 12 Chinese zodiac animals. Their sequence was to be decided by their places in the contest.

News of the contest spread far and wide. The animals who came for registration formed a long queue.

The contest produced many interesting stories.

Story One

The Cat and the Rat Become Enemies

Once upon a time, the cat and the rat were close friends. The cat always stayed in bed every morning until the rat woke him up. On the eve of the contest, the cat urged the rat time and again to wake him up the next morning. The rat readily agreed. The next morning, the rat got up very early and saw the cat still sound asleep. Instead of waking him up, the rat snuck away and hit the road on his own. The cat eventually woke up late and missed the contest. From then on, the cat harbored hatred towards the rat. The cat would chase rats at any sight of one.

Story Two

The Simple-minded Ox

As the rat was rushing to the contest, he encountered the old ox. The clever rat quickly ran to the ox and begged him to help him cross the river. He promised that he wouldn't compete against the ox for first place. The kind, but simple-minded ox agreed and asked the rat to sit on his head. The contest began and he used all of his strength to swim to the other side of the river. As they were approaching the bank, the rat exerted himself and jumped on shore. He then ran towards the finish line before the ox had even reached the riverbank. The rat was the winner while the ox came second in the contest.

Story Three

The Dragon Fails to Become Champion

The dragon had dominion over all the waters and was quite adept at swimming, so how did he fail to become champion? It turned out that right before his departure, he found the land to the west of a mountain was suffering from a drought and the crops people planted were withering. Therefore, the conscientious dragon set off for the Eastern Sea to first fetch water and provide some timely rain for the area west of the mountain. Consequently, he was late for the contest and came in fifth place.

Story Four

The Smart Little Rabbit

Since the rabbit was not a good swimmer, he needed to find another way to cross the river. The quick-witted rabbit hit upon a great idea just one day before the contest: He took a long rope and tied one end of it to a tree on the bank; then he asked the turtle to tie the other end to another tree across the river. When the contest started, the rabbit grabbed the rope and crawled to the other side of the river. He crossed the river without even getting his fur wet.

Story Five

The Goat, the Monkey and the Rooster Help Each Other

The goat, the monkey and the rooster formed a team to help each other cross the river. They found some bamboo poles and ropes and used them to make a raft; then they made two wooden oars out of a plank. When the contest kicked off, the rooster stood in the front to guide the direction while the monkey and the goat sat side by side and paddled hard with the oars. Thanks to their concerted efforts, the three crossed the wide river very quickly.

Story Six

The Last Winner

Many contestants had crossed the river and arrived at the Heavenly Palace. The zodiac official counted but found there were only 11 animals present. Everyone thus kept a close eye on who would turn up as the last winner. Suddenly, a snort was heard — a little pig was coming. The official looked at the pig who was gasping for breath and asked, "Why are you so late?" The pig blushed with shame and replied, "I'm fond of eating and sleeping, which made me grow so fat that I'm no match for them in swimming." Hearing what the pig said, everybody burst into laughter.

申

Perfect Ending

The Jade Emperor announced the contest result: the 12 zodiac animals were sequenced as Rat, Ox, Tiger, Rabbit, Dragon, Snake, Horse, Goat, Monkey, Rooster, Dog and Pig. Since then, the Chinese people have adopted the 12 zodiac animals to designate the years which helped them lead a more regular life and engage in farming appropriately according to seasonal changes.

The Wisdom Behind the Chinese Zodiac Culture

Now let's return from folklore to reality. In fact, an important reason why ancient Chinese selected these 12 animals from the thousands available was perhaps that they had discovered the shining points in each of them.

Confucianism can be viewed as the mainstream of traditional Chinese culture, and the "Doctrine of the Mean" is deemed the essence of Confucianism. By following the "Doctrine of the Mean", or the "Middle Course", the Chinese people strive to be impartial and behave with a sense of propriety. The Chinese idiom过犹不及 (guòyóubùjí), meaning "too much is as bad as too little", can be seen as a good interpretation of the "Doctrine of the Mean". Every coin has two sides. If overdone, a person's strength may take a turn and become his shortcoming. Therefore, by matching the Chinese zodiac animals in pairs, our ancestors were actually hoping to make people aware of their own traits while gaining something from others' strengths in the process of improving themselves. Nowadays, Chinese people hope to work with or marry someone whose personalities are different from their own so as to achieve a balance. In addition, the match of the zodiac animals as shown in the following pages serves as an example to explain the subtle relationship between craftiness and industriousness, bravery and wisdom, low and high profiles, ambition and modesty, resilience and perseverance, and amity and loyalty in traditional Chinese culture.

No. One

Rat and Ox

The rat is known for its quick wit and vigilance; the ox is characterized by its honesty and diligence. As a popular Chinese saying goes, "What a cow eats is nothing but grass, but what it produces is milk." Traditional Chinese values praise the rat's resourcefulness while at the same time upholding the ox's spirit of dedication. If a man relies too much on his cunning, he may tend to be an opportunist and not perform actual deeds; if someone buries himself in hard work, yet lacks the use of skill and method, he may labor hard, but to little avail. Therefore, a wise person should be able to combine his resourcefulness and diligence.

No. Two

Tiger and Rabbit

In Chinese folklore, the tiger has long been regarded as the king of all animals and the epitome of bravery and courage; the little rabbit is a representative of small and weak animals and is known for its prudence and intellect. If a person always takes reckless actions, his bravery will turn into rudeness and invite trouble sooner or later; however, someone who is overcautious may lack the courage to surmount difficulties, making him a coward who is unable to achieve anything. Therefore, the Chinese people consider bravery and prudence two complementary merits a person should possess.

No. Three

Dragon and Snake

The dragon, the mythical animal created by the ancient Chinese people, has been endowed with supreme power and status. It is often used as a metaphor of someone who is in his palmy days and enjoys the best of his time. The snake has been called the "little dragon" because it was demoted to the earth from heaven for breaking the law. Having lost the status of dragon and omnipotent strength, the snake became a synonym for stoicism and kept a low profile. The transformation between the dragon and the snake can be viewed as a real picture of one's life with both high and low points. The character of these two animals may lead to two extremes, and as such, the match of them is a manifestation of the "Doctrine of the Mean" upheld by the Chinese: avoid arrogance in success; don't lose heart in frustration.

No. Four

Horse and Goat

Since ancient times, the horse has been deemed the epitome of enterprising spirit and accomplishment. Those with such merits are often likened by the Chinese people to a "fine steed", which means they are someone with remarkable talent. The goat is praised for its modesty and kindness. In Chinese, idioms containing the character 马 (mǎ, horse) take up the most proportion of phrases related to the zodiac animals, and the majority of them have the meaning of "marching ahead courageously". The goat usually appears in folk stories featuring the theme of kindness and modesty. Therefore, the Chinese often wish to acquire the qualities of both animals.

No. Five

Monkey and Rooster

Characterized by their intelligence and flexibility, some monkeys may be as smart as toddlers in certain aspects. The rooster crows at dawn all year long in all weather. With no clock to use in ancient times, Chinese farmers often relied on the rooster's crow as their wake-up call. Therefore, in the eyes of the Chinese people, the monkey is the epitome of intelligence and flexibility, while the rooster is seen as a perfect example of perseverance. They uphold the view of "acting according to the changing circumstances" while being aware that only through persistent efforts can one achieve success. Given this, we should try to strike a balance between the monkey's flexibility and the rooster's perseverance.

No. Six

Dog and Pig

As man's best friend, a dog will never leave its master even when faced with hunger and death. Pigs, on the contrary, do not care about choosing a master, but rather indulge in eating and sleeping. As a result, pigs are used to refer to people who go with the flow and those who lead a carefree life. Among the Chinese zodiac animals, the dog is the epitome of loyalty and faithfulness while the pig stands for fortune and luck. The Chinese value the dog's loyalty as well as its merit of not despising the poor and currying favor with the rich; meanwhile, they also have an admiration for the pig as it seems to be endowed with good luck.

Can we say the values of the Chinese people are paradoxical? In fact, such seemingly contradictory values are an essential part of Chinese culture. The aforementioned zodiac pairs fully embody the "art of balance" and the pursuit of perfection in Chinese culture.

The Actual Needs Underlying Zodiac Culture

Some experts believe that recording time is a major factor contributing to the appearance of the 12 zodiac animals. The ancient astronomers used to divide one day into 12 double hours, namely 子时 (zǐshí) , 丑时 (chǒushí) , 寅时 (yínshí) , 卯时 (mǎoshí) , 辰时 (chénshí) , 巳时 (sìshí) , 午时 (wǔshí) , 未时 (wèishí) , 申时 (shēnshí) , 酉时 (yǒushí) , 戌时 (xūshí) , 亥

时 (hàishí) , according to the order of the Earthly Branches. Ancient Chinese selected 12 animals as the zodiac signs and determined their order based on the animals' living habits and routine activities at different times each day.

子时 is from 11:00 pm to 1:00 am the next day. It is in the dead of night, and rats move around rampantly at this time. Hence the Rat (鼠 , shǔ) stands for 子时, and is called 子鼠 (zǐshǔ).

丑时 is from 1:00 am to 3:00 am. Farmers often wake up at this time and feed oxen grass by lamplight. Due to this, the Ox (牛 , niú) corresponds with 丑时, and is called 丑牛 (chǒuniú).

寅时 is from 3:00 am to 5:00 am. The nocturnal tigers are quite ferocious and the ancient Chinese could often hear their howls at this time. Because of this, the Tiger (虎 , hǔ) represents 寅时, and is called 寅虎 (yínhǔ).

卯时 is from 5:00 am to 7:00 am. As the day breaks at this time, rabbits often go out of their burrows to eat the green grass covered with morning dew. Therefore, the Rabbit (兔 , tù) stands for 卯时, and is called 卯兔 (mǎotù).

辰时 is from 7:00 am to 9:00 am. The sun rises and it often

gets foggy at this time. Legend has it that the dragon is fond of riding on clouds and mists which go farther up the sky when the sun rises, representing an upward and promising life. Therefore, the Dragon (龙 , lóng) represents 辰时, and is called 辰龙 (chénlóng).

巳时 is from 9:00 am to 11:00 am. When the fog lifts and the sun rises at this time, the snake often crawls out of its cave to look for food. Therefore, the Snake (蛇 , shé) is also called 巳蛇 (sìshé).

午时 is from 11:00 am to 1:00 pm. The ancient wild horse enjoyed neighing and galloping around at noon before it was tamed by human beings. Therefore, the Horse (马 , mǎ) is called 午马 (wǔmǎ).

未时 is from 1:00 pm to 3:00 pm. Shepherds believe it is best to graze goats at this time, so the ancient Chinese associated this period with the goats and offered the zodiac animal Goat (羊 , yáng) another name: 未羊 (wèiyáng).

申时 is from 3:00 pm to 5:00 pm. This is the time just before sunset when the day becomes cooler, which is why the monkey likes climbing trees and yelping in them at this time. Therefore, 申时

corresponds with the Monkey (猴 , hóu), which is also called 申猴 (shēnhóu).

酉时 is from 5:00 pm to 7:00 pm. As the sun sets at this time, the rooster often wanders around in front of its nest. Therefore, the Rooster (鸡 , jī) is also called 酉鸡 (yǒujī).

戌时 is from 7:00 pm to 9:00 pm. This is the time when people lock their doors after a hard day's work, getting ready to rest, and when a dog often stays in front of a house and guards it. If something unusual occurs, it will bark to alert its master. Therefore, the Dog (狗 , gǒu) can also be called 戌狗 (xūgǒu).

亥时 is from 9:00 pm to 11:00 pm. In the still of night, the sleeping sound of pigs can be heard. Therefore, 亥时 is represented by the Pig (猪 , zhū) , which is also called 亥猪 (hàizhū).

By matching the 12 double hours with their corresponding animals, the 12 zodiac animals came into being: Rat, Ox, Tiger, Rabbit, Dragon, Snake, Horse, Goat, Monkey, Rooster, Dog and Pig. Thereafter, ancient Chinese adopted the 12 zodiac animals to record time and years. Since then, a rich culture associated with the 12 zodiac animals has gradually evolved.

Zodiac Animals and the Corresponding 12 Earthly Branches

No.	Earthly Branch	Zodiac Animal
1	*zi* 子	Rat 鼠
2	*chou* 丑	Ox 牛
3	*yin* 寅	Tiger 虎
4	*mao* 卯	Rabbit 兔
5	*chen* 辰	Dragon 龙
6	*si* 巳	Snake 蛇
7	*wu* 午	Horse 马
8	*wei* 未	Goat 羊
9	*shen* 申	Monkey 猴
10	*you* 酉	Rooster 鸡
11	*xu* 戌	Dog 狗
12	*hai* 亥	Pig 猪

第二章 中国12生肖文化起源与内涵

一、中国古代纪年法

中国人很早就创造了历法。大约在中国的夏朝（约公元前2070—公元前1600）时就拥有较为准确的历法，因此，中国传统历法被称为夏历。但夏历并不是用来纪年，而是用来纪月、指导安排农业生产和各种祭祀活动的。大约从西周(公元前1046—公元前771)时期开始，才渐渐形成三种主要的纪年方法：帝王年号纪年法、干支纪年法和生肖纪年法。

第一种纪年法是采用帝王的年号纪年。中国采用帝王年号纪年法始于西汉汉武帝(公元前140—公元前88在位)。起初，一位皇帝可以使用多个年号，汉武帝在位时期就用过11个年号。到了明清时期，才逐渐演变为一位皇帝一个年号。新皇帝登基第二年启用新年号纪年，直至皇帝退位或去世。这种纪年法一直持续到1912年中国清王朝最后一个皇帝——溥仪退位（纪年年号为“宣统”），才随着中国封建帝制的结束而永远成为了历史。

第二种纪年法是使用干支纪年。中国古人选取

10种天象作为列举事物的次序号，称为“天干”。其名称分别是“甲、乙、丙、丁、戊、己、庚、辛、壬、癸”。中国古人又把木星围绕太阳公转的轨道划分为12个部分，称为“地支”。其名称分别是“子、丑、寅、卯、辰、巳、午、未、申、酉、戌、亥”。10个天干与12个地支排列组合数为60，于是干支纪年法就以60年为一个循环周期。纪年从甲子开始，以癸亥结束，周而复始。

第三种纪年法是用12个生肖动物纪年。中国民间大约从汉朝（公元前206—公元220）就开始使用12生肖来纪年了。12年一循环。以12种生肖动物来纪年简单易记、形象生动。每人因出生年而自然对应一种动物，由此中国人创造出内容丰富、独具特色的生肖文化。

1949年中华人民共和国成立后，中国官方开始采用国际上通用的公元纪年法。中国民间则依然盛行生肖纪年法，自古沿用至今。比如公元2010年，在中国民间就纪为虎年，下一个虎年将是2022年。

二、中国12生肖的来历传说

中国人的祖先为什么挑选鼠、牛、虎、兔、龙、蛇、马、羊、猴、鸡、狗、猪这12种动物作为生肖动物呢？顺序又是如何排定的呢？在中国民间，流传着一个家喻户晓的传说故事。

一天，天神太白金星向玉皇大帝（中国神话中天庭和人间所有鬼神的总首领）报告，人间的老百姓没有计算年月的方法，他建议制定一个简单易行的纪年方法，以方便天下百姓按照时节耕种、收获庄稼。玉皇大帝认为这个建议非常好。于是他任命一名生肖官，负责组织一场动物过河比赛，最先过河到达天宫的12种动物会被册封为12生肖，生肖的排位顺序按照比赛名次确定。

渡河比赛获胜可以成为12生肖的消息很快传开，前来报名的动物们排起了长长的队伍。

在比赛过程中发生了许多有趣的小故事。

故事1：猫与老鼠结仇

猫和老鼠本来是一对形影不离的好朋友。平时，猫总爱睡懒觉，早上都是老鼠叫它起床。比赛前一天晚上，猫再三叮嘱老鼠明早记着叫醒它，老鼠满口答应了。第二天早晨，老鼠早早地就起了床，看了看还在熟睡的猫，却没有叫醒它，自己悄悄地上路了。猫醒来后没有赶上生肖比赛，从此就恨上了老鼠，见老鼠就抓。

故事2：憨厚老牛上当

老鼠在急匆匆去参加比赛的路上碰到了老牛。机灵的老鼠急忙跑到老牛身边，可怜兮兮地请求老牛帮助它渡河，还信誓旦旦地保证决不跟老牛抢第一名！善良憨厚的老牛答应了老鼠的请求，让老鼠坐到它的头上。比赛开始了，老牛使出全身力气向河对岸游去。在临近河岸时，没等老牛上岸，老鼠"嗖"的一声第一个跳上了岸，一溜烟似的跑了。老鼠成了第一名，老牛只好屈居第二。

故事3：龙痛失冠军

掌管水务、最擅长游泳的龙为什么没能取得第一名呢？原来龙在临出发前，发现大山以西土地干旱，老百姓的庄稼都快干死了。于是，负责任的龙先到东海取水，再到大山之西去降雨，等赶回来参加比赛时已经迟到了，所以龙只取得第五名的成绩。

故事4：小兔巧妙过河

那么，小兔子不擅长游泳，该怎么过河呢？爱动脑筋的小兔子终于在比赛的前一天想出了一个好方法：它找来一条长长的绳子，先把绳子拴在河边的一棵树上，再请河龟帮忙把绳子的另一头拴在河对岸的另一棵树上。第二天比赛时，小兔子紧紧抓住这条绳子，顺着绳子爬过了河，没有沾到一滴水。

故事5：山羊、猴子和公鸡团队合作

山羊、猴子和公鸡结成团队，共同想办法过河。它们找来一些竹竿和细绳，做成竹筏，用木板做成两支划水的木桨。比赛时，公鸡站在竹筏前头引导方向，猴子和山羊坐在竹筏的左右两边，用木桨使劲划水。它们齐心协力，很快就渡过了宽宽的大河。

故事6：最后一名幸运者

参赛的动物们先后渡过了河，到达了天宫。生肖官仔细一数，只有11种动物。于是，大家都伸长了脖子，想看看到底是谁将幸运地得到这最后一个名额。突然，大家听见“哼、哼”的声音，原来是小猪来了。生肖官看着气喘吁吁的小猪，问道：“你为什么来得这么晚啊？”小猪不好意思地回答说：“我平时贪吃，又爱睡觉，身体有点胖，所以游泳比不过它们。”大家都哈哈大笑了起来。

完美结局

玉皇大帝郑重地宣布比赛结果：12 生肖排名依次是鼠、牛、虎、兔、龙、蛇、马、羊、猴、鸡、狗、猪。从此，人间的百姓就有了用 12 生肖纪年的方法，生活起居有规律，播种和收获庄稼、菜蔬、花木等皆有时节。

三、中国生肖文化的内涵与智慧

现在，我们从 12 生肖动物渡河比赛的神话故事中回归现实。中国古人从千百种常见动物中选定这 12 种动物的重要原因，或许是看中这 12 种动物身上各具不同的优点。

简单来说，中国传统文化的主流是儒家文化，儒家文化的核心内容是“中庸之道”。中庸之道追求不偏不倚、恰到好处，中国成语“过犹不及”便是中庸思想的准确阐释。任何事物都是相对的，即使是优点，过了头便成为了缺点。为此，中国古人依据12个生肖动物的习性特点，将其两两匹配成对，提醒每个人在追求完善自身性格时，需要学习、借鉴其他生肖的性格特点来平衡自身的性格缺陷。在工作和生活中，中国人也希望通过选择与自身性格互补的工作搭档或异性伴侣，让两种看似对立的性格加以中和，实现平衡，以达到完美的境界。这种生肖匹配还具体解释了中国传统文化观念中关于取巧与勤奋、勇敢与理智、高调与低调、进取与谦虚、权变与坚持、随和与忠诚的微妙关系。

1. 鼠和牛配对

老鼠聪明伶俐、机警灵活。老牛的特点则是踏实勤恳、埋头苦干，中国人最喜欢用这样一句谚语来评价牛的奉献精神："吃的是草，挤出的是奶。"在中国传统文化价值观里，人们既欣赏老鼠的机智取巧，又推崇老牛的踏实苦干精神。如果头脑过于灵活，容易不喜欢干实事，走向投机取巧；如果只埋头苦干，不懂得做事的技巧和方法，就会事倍功半。因此聪明的头脑和勤奋能干的品质二者应完美统一。

2. 虎和兔配对

在中国民间故事里，老虎历来是百兽之王，是勇敢的王者化身。而小兔代表弱小动物，谨慎、理智。如果凡事无所顾忌，勇敢也会变成鲁莽，容易闯祸；而事事过分谨慎，就会缺少克服困难的勇气，就会变得懦弱，无所作为。因此，中国人认为勇敢和谨慎是相辅相成的一对好兄弟。

3. 龙和蛇配对

中国人赋予中华民族创造的神物——“龙”以无上的地位和能力，龙代表的是春风得意和高调。而蛇则是被天庭降罪贬罚到人间的“小龙”，并且丧失了龙的地位和力量，因此蛇成为隐忍、低调的代表。龙和蛇的转换表现出有高潮、有低谷的真实人生，两者的性格特点代表了两个方向，将龙与蛇配对反映出中国人信奉的中庸信条：得志不应骄傲，失意不应颓废。

4. 马和羊配对

自古以来，在中国人的观念中，马是“勇往直前、马到成功”的典型形象。中国人经常把具备这样特点的人比喻为“千里马”，即千里挑一、难得一见的人才。而羊被中国人称道的优秀品质则是谦逊、平和。在汉语中，含有“马”字的成语可能是12生肖动物中最多的，而且绝大多数具有“勇往直前”的意思。羊则是中国民间关于“善良与谦虚”主题故事的主角。因此，中国人希望把马的勇往直前与羊的谦虚平和完美结合起来。

5. 猴和鸡配对

猴子轻巧灵活、善于变化，其智商与人类最接近。而公鸡无论天气如何，一年365天，每到黎明时分就会打鸣。在古代，中国农民缺少计时工具，往往就以公鸡打鸣作为晨起的信号。因此，中国人把猴子视为灵活权变的典型代表，而公鸡则是持之以恒的代表。中国人一方面赞赏视环境条件不同而随机应变的为人处世观，另一方面又主张持之以恒才能做出成就，所以认为猴的灵活权变与鸡的持之以恒可以和谐互补。

6. 狗和猪配对

狗对主人十分忠诚，宁可饿死也不会抛弃主人。猪呢，不择主人，只求吃饱睡好，是顺其自然、随遇而安的典型。在中国生肖文化中，狗是忠诚、专一的代表，猪则是财富和幸运的代名词。中国人既推崇狗忠诚而不爱富嫌贫的品质，又羡慕猪不费力气就不愁吃喝的幸运。

中国人的价值观是不是有些矛盾呢？可是，这样的矛盾价值观却是中国文化中不可缺少的重要内容。12种动物的配对，充分体现出中国文化的平衡智慧与追求完美的价值取向。

四、中国生肖文化诞生的现实需求

一些专家认为，12生肖产生的原因主要是出于记时的需要。古代天文学家将一昼夜分为12个时辰，每个时辰为两个小时，并按照地支的顺序分别命名为“子时、丑时、寅时、卯时、辰时、巳时、午时、未时、申时、酉时、戌时、亥时”。中国古人就依照生活中观察到不同时间段内动物的行为习惯和活动规律，确定了12生肖的顺序。

夜间11点至次日凌晨1点，属子时，正是老鼠趁夜深人静频繁活动之时。因此，子时对应生肖动物为鼠，故称“子鼠”。

凌晨1点至3点，属丑时。牛习惯夜间吃草，农民就会在深夜起床来挑灯喂牛。因此，丑时对应生肖动物为牛，故称“丑牛”。

凌晨3点至5点，属寅时。此时昼伏夜行的老虎最凶猛，古人经常会在这个时段听到虎啸声。因此，寅时对应生肖动物为虎，故称“寅虎”。

清晨5点至7点，属卯时。兔子喜欢吃带有晨露的青草，所以天刚亮它们就出窝了。因此，卯时对应生肖动物为兔，故称“卯兔”。

早晨7点至9点，属辰时。此时一般容易起雾，又值旭日东升、蒸蒸日上之时，而传说中龙最喜腾云驾雾。因此，人们把辰时留给了龙，称此时为“辰龙”。

上午9点至11时，属巳时。此时大雾散去，艳阳高照，蛇类出洞觅食，故称“巳蛇”。

中午11点至1点，属午时。古时野马尚未被人类驯服，喜欢午时四处奔跑嘶鸣，故将此时称为“午马”。

午后1点至3点，属未时。牧羊人认为这是放羊的好时候。因此，古人就把未时与羊对应，称此时为“未羊”。

下午3点至5点，属申时。此时太阳偏西了，天气凉爽，猴子喜欢在此时爬树啼叫。因此，申时对应生肖动物为猴，故称“申猴”。

下午5点至7点，属酉时。此时太阳落山了，鸡在窝前打转，故称“酉鸡”。

傍晚7点至9点，属戌时。人们劳碌一天，闩门准备休息了。狗卧门前守护，一有动静就汪汪大叫以警示主人，故称此时为“戌狗”。

夜间9点至11点，属亥时。夜深人静，人们能听见猪酣睡的声音，于是将亥时与猪对应，称作“亥猪”。

一天的12个时辰与12个生肖动物就这样匹配排列下来：子鼠、丑牛、寅虎、卯兔、辰龙、巳蛇、午马、未羊、申猴、酉鸡、戌狗、亥猪。于是中国古人开始使用12生肖对应一昼夜计时，后来又使用12生肖来纪年，从而衍生出丰富多彩的12生肖文化。

Chapter Three

A Kaleidoscope of Tiger References

Evolution of the Chinese Character 虎 (Tiger)

The evolution of Chinese characters has undergone several phases, namely, the Oracle Bone Script, Bronze Inscriptions, Lesser Seal Script, Clerical Script, Cursive Script, Regular Script and Running Script.

Ancient Chinese characters underwent drastic transformations with changes in writing materials. At the very beginning, characters were inscribed on tortoise shells and animal bones, hence the name 甲骨文 (jiǎgǔwén , the Oracle Bone Script), literally "shell and bone script". Subsequently, in the Zhou Dynasty (1046-256 BC), people inscribed characters on bronze objects which gave birth to and even popularized Bronze Inscriptions to a certain extent. Later on, China split up into seven states (Qi, Chu, Qin, Yan, Zhao, Wei, Han), each with its own characters. When the State of Qin grew in power, it defeated the other six states and unified China. In order to consolidate his rule, the First Emperor of the Qin Dynasty ordered a cancellation of all the characters of the other six states and introduced a unified Chinese character style: the Lesser Seal Script. Like the Oracle Bone Script and Bronze Inscriptions, this writing style still involved complicated characters that were difficult to write. Moreover, people wrote on bamboo slips and wooden boards that were not convenient to carry. According to the historical records, when Dongfang Shuo, a renowned minister during the Western Han Dynasty (206 BC-AD 25), submitted a proposal to the emperor, the bamboo slips were so heavy that they had to be carried by two men into the palace. With the passage of time, Clerical Script came into being, which can be seen as a more concise version of Lesser Seal Script. This marked a major evolution of Chinese characters. With the introduction of Clerical Script, ancient Chinese characters started their transformation into modern styles. Cursive Script, Regular Script, and Running Script developed from Clerical Script and are considered the major character styles of Chinese calligraphy. In the year 105 during the Eastern Han Dynasty, a eunuch official named Cai Lun invented the technology that led to the widespread use of paper for writing. Thanks to the introduction of paper, Chinese calligraphy has become an established and popular art form.

Oracle Bone Script

Bronze Inscriptions

Lesser Seal Script

In Oracle Bone Script, the Chinese character for "tiger" resembles a fierce tiger with its mouth wide open. This is a typical pictograph.

Cursive Script

Clerical Script

Regular Script

Running Script

Although the fundamental construction of the character as a pictograph has not changed throughout its long evolution, the form it took in Oracle Bone Script and Bronze Inscriptions differs a lot from what it looks like today. The character was greatly simplified during the Lesser Seal Script period, and its current form essentially took shape during the Clerical Script period.

	Oracle Bone Script	Shang Dynasty (1600-1046 BC).
	Bronze Inscriptions	The Spring and Autumn Period and the Warring States Period (770-221 BC).
	Lesser Seal Script	Qin Dynasty (221-206 BC) and Western Han Dynasty.
	Cursive Script	Began in the Western Han Dynasty and became widely used during the Eastern Han Dynasty, the Sui Dynasty (581-618), and the Tang Dynasty.
	Clerical Script	Widely used at the end of the Western Han Dynasty.
	Regular Script	Began at the end of the Eastern Han Dynasty, became widely used during the period of the Three Kingdoms, the Jin Dynasty (265-420) and the Southern and Northern Dynasties (420-589), and reached its peak during the Tang Dynasty.
	Running Script	Began at the end of the Eastern Han Dynasty, matured during the period of the Three Kingdoms, the Jin Dynasty and the Southern and Northern Dynasties.

Tiger-related Idioms, Proverbs, Allegorical Sayings and a Nursery Rhyme

In Chinese, you can find a lot of idioms, proverbs and allegorical sayings containing the character 虎.

I. A selection of tiger-related idioms

1. 狐假虎威

① **Pinyin:** hújiǎ-hǔwēi

② **Literal translation: a fox assuming the majesty of a tiger**

③ **Meaning: bully people by flaunting one's powerful connections**

The idiom originally told of a fox that took advantage of a tiger's ferocity to scare away other beasts. Later, it came to mean relying on somebody else's strength to bully or intimidate others.

This idiom is derived from a fable wherein a tiger, who is the king of the forest, goes hunting and catches a fox. Fearing it would be eaten, the fox lies to the tiger, saying, "You can't eat me. I am a messenger from God of Heaven!" The tiger was uncertain about the fox's claim, so in order to dispel the tiger's doubt, the fox continued, "If you don't believe this, just follow me. I'll show you that all the beasts in the forest will run and hide out of fear when they come across me." Of course, when the tiger walked with the fox through the forest, all the animals fled in fear of the tiger, not the fox. In other words, the mighty tiger was fooled by the cunning fox. As a result, the tiger set the fox free.

2. 马马虎虎

① **Pinyin: mǎmǎhūhū**

② **Literal translation: a tiger-horse painting**

③ **Meaning: careless, sloppy**

This idiom comes from a story of a painter in the Song Dynasty (960-1279). The painter lived in the capital and was notorious for the sloppiness of his painting. One day, he worked at home on a painting of a tiger. When he had just finished the tiger's head, a guest came to visit him, asking him to paint a horse. Hearing the request, the painter simply drew a horse's body attached to the tiger's head. Seeing this tiger-horse painting, the guest was so angry that he left without taking it. The painter then hung the picture in his living room. Seeing the picture, his eldest son asked him what the animal in the painting was. He said it was a tiger. On another occasion, his youngest son asked the same question. He told him it was a horse. Before long, his eldest son went hunting and shot dead a horse which he mistook for a tiger. He then had to pay its owner lots of money in compensation. Several days later, his youngest son, while hiking in the suburbs, saw a tiger. He thought it was a horse and went to ride it. Unsurprisingly, he was killed by the beast. The painter was so remorseful that he burned the painting and wrote a poem exhorting others to learn from his mistake.

3. 苛政猛于虎

① **Pinyin:** kēzhèng měng yú hǔ

② **Literal translation: Tyranny is fiercer than a tiger.**

③ **Meaning: A tyrannical government is more to be feared than ferocious tigers.**

This idiom is related to Confucius. It is said that sometime during his travels around the states, Confucius saw a woman weeping sadly in front of a grave at the foot of Mount Taishan. Confucius stopped his chariot and sent his disciple Zilu to ask the woman why she was crying. "You are weeping so intensely. You must be in much grief," Zilu said. The woman nodded, "This is true. My father-in-law was killed by a tiger, so was my husband. Now my son has also died in the same way!" Confucius asked in bewilderment, "Why do you still stay here?" "Because we don't suffer from harsh policies here," came the reply.

Confucius was deeply moved, and he said to his disciples, "You should bear in mind that harsh rules are even more fearful than tigers!"

4. 不入虎穴，焉得虎子

① **Pinyin:** bú rù hǔxué, yān dé hǔ zǐ

② **Literal translation: How can you catch tiger cubs**

without entering a tiger's lair?

③ Meaning: nothing ventured, nothing gained

This idiom has its origin in the story of Ban Chao (32-102), a renowned military strategist and diplomat in the Eastern Han Dynasty who made great contributions in the war against the nomadic Xiongnu people. Ban Chao was dispatched by Emperor Mingdi as an ambassador to the Kingdom of Shanshan (in present-day Xinjiang) to form an alliance with it to mutually resist the Xiongnu invasion. After a long and arduous journey, he and his entourage finally arrived at their destination, where they were warmly received and treated as guests of honor. Hearing his intention, the King of Shanshan was very glad.

A few days later, however, the Xiongnu people also sent envoys to talk with the king.They all spoke ill of the Eastern Han government before the king, who became scared and worried. The next day, he refused to meet with Ban, giving him the cold shoulder. He even sent troops to watch Ban and his men.

Realizing that the situation was critical, Ban immediately assembled his men to develop countermeasures. He believed that the situation was dire and that only by getting rid of the Xiongnu envoys could they dispel the king's misgivings and restore friendship between the two countries.

At the time, Ban did not have many men and weapons, while the Xiongnu soldiers were strong and their defenses were staunch. However, Ban encouraged his men, saying, "How can you catch tiger cubs without entering a tiger's lair?" Late that night, Ban led his soldiers to the camp of the Xiongnu people. There, he divided his men in two groups. One group beat drums and yelled outside the camp while the other group prowled into the camp and set fire to the tents. The Xiongnu soldiers woke up with a start and were totally disoriented. In a state of panic and chaos, they were either killed by the fire or shot dead by the archers who lay in ambush outside the camp. Seeing this, the King of Shanshan realized that he had offended the Xiongnu people. Daring not to offend the Han court, he had to reconcile with Ban.

5. 坐山观虎斗

① **Pinyin:** zuò shān guān hǔ dòu

② **Literal translation: sit on top of a mountain to watch two tigers fight**

It means one can watch safely others fight and then reap the spoils when both sides are exhausted.

6. 两虎相争，必有一伤

① **Pinyin:** liǎng hǔ xiāng zhēng , bì yǒu yì shāng

② **Literal translation: When two tigers fight, one is sure to get hurt.**

This means that when two strong opponents fight, one side will invariably end up seriously wounded.

II. A selection of tiger-related proverbs

Chinese proverbs originated from the people. They are popular and simple fixed sayings that have deep meanings. They are often used in spoken language to achieve a more vivid, expressive and accurate effect.

1. 虎毒不食子

① **Pinyin:** hǔ dú bù shí zǐ

② **Literal translation: Ferocious as it is, a tigress never eats its cubs.**

This proverb is quite popular in China. Though a tigress is

fierce and feared by other beasts, due to its strong maternal love, it would choose to starve to death over eating its own cubs. The proverb is used as a metaphor to reflect parents' profound love for their children.

2. 虎落平阳被犬欺

① **Pinyin:** hǔ luò píngyáng bèi quǎn qī

② **Literal translation: A tiger in the plain may get bullied even by a dog.**

If a tiger comes to the plain from a forest or mountainous area, it will become vulnerable and even a dog can bully it. It is used as a metaphor to indicate the fact that advantages can turn into disadvantages when conditions change.

III. A selection of tiger-related allegorical sayings

Allegorical sayings consist of two parts. The first part serves as a clue to a riddle and the second part as its solution. Under some circumstances, people can figure out the meaning with the clue even without the second part. Therefore, the second part can often be omitted when allegorical sayings are used, hence, the literal meaning of allegorical saying in Chinese is "the expression that can take a break (in the middle)".

1. 老虎爬树——不会这一套

① **Pinyin:** lǎohǔ páshù — bú huì zhè yí tào

② **Meaning: Tree-climbing to a tiger — beyond one's capability**

This allegorical saying is predicated upon the fact that the tiger is one of the few feline species that are not adept at climbing trees. Therefore, it is used to refer to the skills people do not possess or are not good at.

2. 老虎嘴里拔牙——凶多吉少

① **Pinyin:** lǎohǔ zuǐ li bá yá — xiōngduō-jíshǎo

② **Meaning: To pull a tooth from a tiger's mouth — bode ill rather than well**

This saying is used to indicate how people's risky actions always bode ill rather than well.

IV. A tiger-related nursery rhyme

Chinese oral literature and music are full of animal imagery. The following nursery rhyme is called "Two Tigers". It is extremely popular in China. "Two Tigers" has simple lyrics and a beautiful melody. A literal translation of its lyrics is as follows:

Two tigers, two tigers,

Running fast, running fast.

One has no ears;

One has no tail.

It's so weird.

It's so weird.

Tiger-related Chinese Stories

I. The tiger learns new skills

This is an interesting folk story that is known far and wide in China. Its abridged version is as follows:

The tiger and the cat looked alike because they were cousins.

But unlike the cat, the tiger had no hunting skills. He couldn't catch prey and would often go hungry. Meanwhile, the cat was agile and good at hunting. He never went hungry.

One day, after yet again failing to capture anything to eat, the tiger decided to approach the cat and ask him to teach him how to hunt.

Initially, the cat would not agree to do this. But the tiger pleaded persistently, and the cat finally gave in. However, the cat only agreed to pass on the hunting skills if the tiger were to follow three rules. First, the tiger had to endure hardships without taking shortcuts. Second, he couldn't pass on the hunting skills to others once he had gained them. Third, he was not allowed to bully others with the skills he mastered.

Then, the cat began to teach the tiger a variety of skills, which the tiger learned diligently. These skills included dashing, landing and pouncing.

Dashing was mainly used for launching a sudden attack; that is to chase prey as fast as a gust of wind. The cat master taught the tiger how to quietly approach prey and make a dash for it.

After one month of study, the tiger was able to approach prey like the cat. He could charge at speeds as fast as his master.

Landing refers to the ability to land safely when jumping from a height. The cat master told the tiger to keep calm, use the tail for balance, and let the claws of the front legs land first. Using this technique, the jumper could be cushioned without getting hurt. After one month of painstaking practice, the tiger could make a safe landing after jumping from a high place.

Pouncing is to take down prey with the front paws, ensuring there would be no escape. Through a month of patient and repeated practice, the tiger was able to easily catch a lot of prey with this trick.

Having acquired these skills, the tiger became the strongest animal in the forest, and he was elected king of all beasts.

After a while, the tiger gradually became so conceited that he showed little respect to his cat master. Moreover, he worried that the cat would teach others the skills he now possessed, so he decided to get rid of him.

One day, upon seeing the cat, the tiger threw himself at the cat.

The cat quickly turned to flee, and the tiger desperately chased after him. At the critical moment when the tiger was about to catch him, the cat climbed up a tall poplar tree on the side of the road. The tiger was left alone under the big tree, totally at a loss as to what he should do.

It turned out that the cat had withheld one skill when he was teaching the tiger. He did not teach the tiger how to climb a tree. This is the age-old story about how a tiger learned hunting skills from a cat. Interestingly, the tiger is indeed among the rare feline animals that are not good at climbing trees.

II. Wu Song fights the tiger

This story is well-known among Chinese people. It is from *Outlaws of the Marsh*, one of the four classic Chinese novels. The novel portrays how Song Jiang led a group of heroes and heroines to launch a peasant uprising during the Song Dynasty. Wu Song is a typical example of these characters — a hero who smote a tiger to death.

Here is an abridged version of the story:

Having been away from his home for years, Wu Song decided

to go home to visit his elder brother, Wu Dalang, who had raised him. On the way home, he passed by Jingyang Ridge in Yanggu County (present-day Liaocheng City, Shandong Province) where he drank 18 bowls of liquor in a hostel. The waiter strongly urged him not to walk through the ridge alone because of a ferocious tiger on the mountain. Wu Song defied his warning, believing it was a trick and the man was trying to scare him into staying at the hostel. So he continued his journey and staggered on the mountain.

At sunset, he arrived at a dilapidated temple and saw a government notice on its gate. Reading the notice, Wu Song finally realized that there was indeed a ferocious tiger on the mountain. He considered going back to the hostel, but dismissed the idea, as people at the hostel might mock him. So he moved on. Before long, the alcohol kicked in and he became sleepy. He found a large flat rock to lie down on and just as he was about to fall asleep, he suddenly heard a gust of wind. It was a fierce tiger rushing towards him. Wu Song was startled, and he quickly broke out in a cold sweat. He evaded the tiger swiftly and jumped behind it. The animal turned and attempted to pounce again, but Wu Song dodged it once more. The tiger was enraged. With a roar, it swept its tail at Wu Song, but he quickly leaped away. While the beast was turning to aim

another attack, Wu Song swung a wooden club that he carried with him at the tiger, striking out towards the tiger's head with all his might. Unfortunately, the club hit a tree branch and broke it with a crash. Provoked, the tiger became even more savage.

It attempted to pounce once more, but Wu Song ducked yet again. Dropping the broken club, he mounted the beast in the blink of an eye. He grabbed hold of the tiger's coat with one hand while repeatedly punching the tiger's head with the other. The tiger was beaten so badly that it eventually lay still on its stomach with its eyes, mouth, nose and ears bleeding. Fearing that the tiger might feign death, Wu Song picked up the broken club and beat the tiger with it until he was sure that it was no longer breathing.

Sometime later, local hunters found Wu Song and the dead tiger. They reported his exploits to the government immediately. From then on, Wu Song became well-known across the country as the "tiger-fighter hero".

鼠　牛　虎　兔

龙　蛇　马　羊

猴　鸡　狗　猪

十二生肖

第三章 生肖虎趣谈

一、“虎”的字形演变

简单总结中国文字的演变，大致经历了甲骨文—金文—小篆—隶书—草书—楷书—行书等阶段。

中国古文字的变迁是伴随着书写载体的变化而变化的。最早人们把文字刻在龟甲兽骨上，所以称为“甲骨文”。后来到了周朝时期，人们在金属钟鼎器具上铸文，金文出现并得到一定推广。周朝后期，中国开始动荡，逐渐分裂成七个诸侯国，每个诸侯国都有自己的文字。后来秦国逐渐强大起来，并最终战胜六国，统一了中国。为了便于统治，秦朝第一个皇帝——秦始皇取消其他六国的文字，创制了统一的汉字书写形式，即小篆。小篆与甲骨文、金文字形一样，仍然很复杂，书写不易；加之当时的人们一般是在竹简、木板上书写，十分不方便。史书记载，中国西汉时期的名臣东方朔给皇帝提的建议写成竹简需要两个成年男子抬进皇宫去。这种情况下，小篆渐渐向简便快捷的方向演变，逐渐形成了隶书。采用隶书在中国汉字发展史上是一个重大的变革，从隶书开始，古代汉字的字形基本接近于现代汉字。后来中国书法作品主要的字体形式草书、楷书、行书均从隶书演化而成。公元105年，中国东汉宦官蔡伦发明造纸术，纸张自此逐渐被广泛应用。因为纸张的使用，中国书法才得以成为一门普及而成熟的艺术门类。

汉字“虎”在甲骨文中就有，字形就是一只逼真的老虎，虎口大张，足尾完整，属于典型的象形字。

虽然“虎”字在漫长岁月演变中并未改变其象形字的根本，但是今天的汉字“虎”与甲骨文和金文中的“虎”字已差别很大。“虎”字在小篆时期得以大幅简化，到隶书时期基本确立了今天汉字“虎”的雏形。

	甲骨文	商朝
	金文	先秦时期
	小篆	秦、西汉
	草书	始于西汉，兴盛于东汉、隋唐
	隶书	兴于西汉末期
	楷书	始于汉末，兴于三国两晋南北朝，盛于唐朝
	行书	始于汉末，成熟于三国两晋南北朝

二、与虎相关的成语、谚语、歇后语和儿歌

在汉语中，含有“虎”字的成语、民间谚语和歇后语不在少数。

1. 与虎相关的成语

（1）狐假虎威

本意是狐狸假借老虎的威风去吓唬其他野兽。

后来比喻倚仗别人的势力来欺压或吓唬人。

这个成语出自一个寓言故事。森林之王老虎饥肠辘辘，正在四处寻找猎物，恰巧逮住了狐狸。狐狸怕被老虎吃掉，就编造谎言欺骗老虎说：“你不能吃我，我是天帝派来的使者！”老虎半信半疑。狐狸为了打消老虎的疑虑，就说：“如果你不信，就请你跟在我后面，看一看森林里的百兽是不是看到我就会吓得四处逃窜。”结果事情正像狐狸所说的那样，老虎只好放走了狐狸。其实，森林里的百兽被吓得四处逃窜是因为看见了老虎而不是狐狸。威猛的老虎上了狡猾狐狸的当。

（2）马马虎虎

形容做事不认真、不仔细，敷衍了事或粗心大意。

这个成语也有一个故事。宋朝时，京城里有位画画儿草率随意的画家。有一次，他在家里画虎，刚刚画好虎头家里就来了一位客人索画儿，请他画一匹马。他就随手在虎头后面画上了马身子。客人一看这幅似马非马的画儿，十分生气，画儿也不要就走了。这位画家就把这幅画儿挂在了自家客厅。大儿子问他画儿里的动物是什么，他说是虎。小儿子问他画儿里的动物是什么，他却说是马。没多久，大儿子出去打猎竟然把别人家的马当成虎给射死了，只好赔了人家很多钱了事。又过了一阵子，小儿子去郊外玩耍时看见一只老虎，他以为是马想去骑，结果被老虎咬死了。画家悔恨万分，写了一首诗自责："马虎图，马虎图，似马又似虎，长子依图射死马，次子依图喂了虎。草堂焚毁马虎图，奉劝诸君莫学吾。"

（3）苛政猛于虎

形容官府繁杂、苛刻的政令比猛虎还要凶残可怕。

这个成语与儒家学说的创始人孔子有关。据说孔子在周游列国时路过泰山脚下，看见一个妇人在坟墓前哭得十分悲伤。孔子停下车，派弟子子路前去询问那个妇人哭泣的原因。子路问道："你哭得那么伤心，应该有很多伤心的事吧？"那个妇人回答说："没错，之前我的公公被老虎咬死了，后来我的丈夫又被老虎咬死了，现在我的儿子也被老虎咬死了！"孔子不解地问道："那你为什么还不离开这里呢？"妇人回答说："因为这里没有严酷的政令。"

孔子十分感慨，对弟子们说：“你们要记住啊，残暴的政令比老虎还要凶猛可怕！”

（4）不入虎穴，焉得虎子

本意是不敢深入老虎的巢穴，怎么能得到虎崽呢！现比喻不亲历危险的境地或者艰苦实践，就不能取得重大的成就。

这个成语也出自一个古代历史故事。班超是中国历史上东汉时期著名军事家、外交家，在当时为朝廷抗击匈奴立下大功。汉明帝派遣班超出使鄯善国（即现在的新疆地区），力求结盟共同抵御匈奴的入侵。班超带着一队人马，一路跋山涉水，千里迢迢来到了鄯善国。鄯善王亲自出城迎候，并把班超奉为座上宾。班超向鄯善王说明来意，鄯善王很高兴。

没想到过了几天，匈奴也派使者来和鄯善王交涉。匈奴人在鄯善王面前说了东汉朝廷许多坏话。鄯善王顿时心绪不安。第二天，他拒不接见班超，态度十分冷淡，甚至派兵监视班超等人。

班超意识到情况不妙，立刻召集大家商量对策。班超认为，当下情况险恶，只有奋力除掉匈奴使者才能消除鄯善王的疑虑，两国和好。

当时班超的人马不多，而匈奴兵强马壮，防守严密。但班超激励大家说："不入虎穴，焉得虎子！"这天深夜，班超亲自带领士兵来到匈奴使者的营地附近。他们兵分两路，一路拿着战鼓在营地外击鼓呐喊，一路潜入营地，并放火烧帐篷。匈奴人从睡梦中惊醒，军心大乱，结果不是被大火烧死，就是被埋伏在营地外的弓箭手乱箭射死。鄯善王看到这种结局，明白已然得罪了匈奴人，不敢再得罪汉朝廷，便和班超言归于好。

（5）坐山观虎斗

本意指坐在山上看老虎相斗。比喻对双方的斗争采取旁观的态度，等到两败俱伤的时候再从中取利。

（6）两虎相争，必有一伤

本意指两只虎相斗，一定会有一只因受伤而败下阵来。比喻两个强者互相搏斗，必然有一方要遭严重损害。

2. 关于虎的谚语

中国谚语是形成于民间的固定语句，用简单通俗的话反映出深刻的道理，多使用在口语中，以增加语言的生动性、形象性和准确性。

（1）虎毒不食子

这是一句在中国流传度很高的谚语，特别能体现中国父母对子女的深厚情感。这句谚语是指老虎虽然凶猛，百兽惧怕，但它护犊的母性极强，即使自己饿死也不吃自己的幼崽。

（2）虎落平阳被犬欺

本意是说老虎离开山林，在平地连狗都可以欺负它。后来比喻条件、环境如发生改变，原来的优势也会变成劣势。

3. 关于虎的歇后语

中国的歇后语由前后两部分组成：前一部分起“引子”的作用，像谜面；后一部分像谜底。在一定的语言环境中，通常当说话者说出前半截，听话者就可以领会和猜想出它的本意，常常可以“歇”去后半截，所以就把这样的句子称为“歇后语”。

（1）老虎爬树——不会这一套

这句歇后语是根据老虎的自身特点总结而来的。因为老虎是猫科动物中少有的不擅爬树的动物之一，所以中国人用“老虎爬树”来形容人不具备或根本不擅长的本事或技能。

（2）老虎嘴里拔牙——凶多吉少

中国人用这句歇后语来形容一些人的冒险举动必然是凶多吉少的结果。

4. 关于虎的儿歌

在民间口头文学和音乐艺术中，动物是不可或缺的重要角色。《两只老虎》应该算是中国儿童传唱度极高的儿歌之一，歌词简单、朗朗上口：

两只老虎，两只老虎，
跑得快，跑得快，
一只没有耳朵，

一只没有尾巴，
真奇怪，真奇怪。

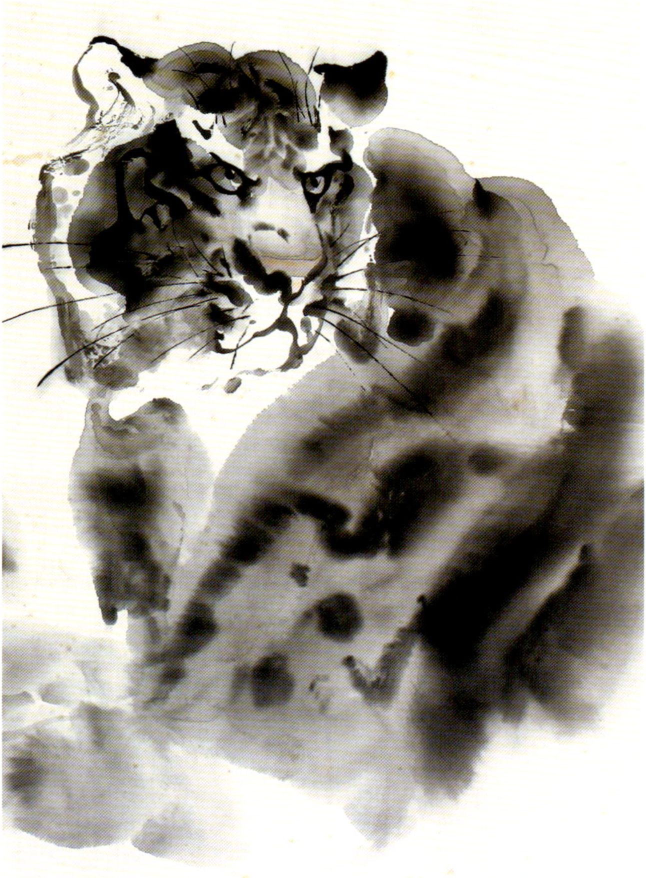

三、关于老虎的中国经典故事

1. 老虎学艺

这是一个在中国民间流传很广的有趣故事。故事梗概如下：

老虎和猫长得很像，因为它们是亲戚，老虎是表哥，猫是表弟。

起初老虎没什么本领，常常因为捕捉不到猎物而饿肚子。猫却身手敏捷，捕猎本领高强。

有一天，老虎捕猎又是一无所获，就下决心拜猫表弟为师学艺。

猫表弟一开始不答应，可是老虎表哥苦苦哀求，猫禁不住老虎的再三央求，就答应了它。但是，猫对老虎学艺约法三章："一是老虎学习本领要不怕吃苦，不能投机取巧；二是老虎不能把本领再教给其他动物；三是老虎学会本领后，不能欺负别的动物。"

从那以后，猫师傅开始教老虎各种本领。老虎也学习得很认真。猫师傅主要教给了老虎三种本

领——跑、跳、扑。

第一项本领是“跑”，名字叫“动如疾风”，主要是练习突然出击，像疾风一样的速度去追捕猎物。猫师傅先教老虎如何悄悄地靠近猎物的技巧，然后教它如何快速奔跑的方法。老虎经过一个多月的学习，终于能够像猫一样悄悄地接近猎物，奔跑起来速度一点也不输给猫师傅了。

第二项本领是“跳”，名字叫“猛虎下山”，主要是练习从高处跳到低处并安全落地的本领。猫师傅告诉老虎从高处跳落的技巧——不能慌张，要用尾巴掌握平衡，让两条前腿的爪尖先着地，然后两条后腿再着地。这样才能减轻冲击力，不会受伤。老虎认真练习这一招，又用了一个月时间，终于练得像猫一样又快又好地从高处跳落了。

第三项本领是“扑”，名字叫“泰山压顶”，主要是练习如何用两个前爪一下子把猎物扑倒在地使它们不能再逃脱的本领。老虎耐心地反复练习，一个月后，它已经能利用这一招轻而易举地捕获许多猎物了。

老虎学成武艺后，那真是如虎添翼，动物们就选它做森林的“百兽之王”。

后来，老虎渐渐骄傲起来，也不再把猫师傅放在眼里了。老虎还担心猫再把这些本领教给别人，就决定找机会吃掉猫。

有一天，老虎正巧碰见了猫，就猛地一跳，两只前爪扑向猫，猫赶紧转身就跑。老虎在后面拼命地追。眼看老虎就要追上了猫，猫一纵身爬上了路边一棵高高的白杨树。老虎围着大树团团转，急得吹胡子瞪眼却没什么好办法。

原来，猫教老虎学艺的时候留了一手，没有把爬树的本领教给老虎。这就是在中国民间流传很久的老虎向猫学艺的故事。事实上，老虎也确实是猫科动物里少有不擅爬树的动物。

2. 武松打虎

武松打虎的故事在中国民间妇孺皆知，这个故事出自中国古典四大名著之一的《水浒传》。书中主要讲述了在宋代宋江领导众多英雄进行农民起义的故事。武松就是其中一个代表人物——打虎英雄。

其故事梗概如下：

侠客武松离开老家很多年后，回家探望把他抚养长大的哥哥武大郎。经过景阳冈时，武松在一家酒馆喝了十八碗酒后要离开时，酒店伙计劝武松不要单独过山岗，因为山上有恶虎伤人，武松却不以为然，认为是伙计吓唬他，依然一个人往山上走去。

走到太阳快落山时，武松来到一破庙前。庙门上贴了一张官府告示，武松读后方知山上真有猛虎。回去住店，又怕被店家笑话，他只好继续向前走。没走多久，由于酒力发作，他便找了一块大青石，仰身躺下。武松刚要入睡，忽听一阵狂风呼啸，一只猛虎朝他扑了过来。武松惊出一身冷汗，急忙一闪身，躲在老虎背后。老虎转过身又猛扑过来，武松又躲了过去。老虎大怒，大吼一声，用尾巴向武松横扫过来。武松急忙跳开，并趁猛虎转身的那一霎间，举起随身带的粗木棒，运足力气，朝虎头猛打下去。只听“咔嚓”一声，木棒打在树枝上折断了。这时，老虎又向武松扑过来，武松扔掉半截木棒，顺势骑在老虎背上，左手揪住老虎头上的皮，右手猛击虎头，没多久就把老虎打得到处流血，趴在地上不能动弹了。武松怕老虎装死，举起半截木棒又打了一阵，见那老虎确实没气了，才住手。

后来，当地的猎人们发现了武松和被他打死的老虎，忙把这件事报告了官府，从此“打虎英雄——武松”名扬天下。

Chapter Four

The Tiger in Chinese Indigenous Art

Tiger-themed Chinese Paintings

I. Chinese Traditional Paintings

The traditional Chinese painting style involves using a water-dipped brush to draw on paper or silk with ink or watercolor. Figures, landscapes, flowers, and birds are common subjects for Chinese traditional, paintings.

Since ancient times, the 12 Chinese zodiac animals have been an important theme for paintings in China. Whenever the Year of the Tiger arrives, the tiger becomes a popular subject for Chinese painters that year.

Chinese people have adored tigers since ancient times. Tiger paintings can be found on the rock faces of many mountains. In some of the excavated tombs of the Han Dynasty, many fine tiger portraits have been found. Throughout history, there have been many Chinese painters known for their tiger paintings, such as Li Jian in the Tang Dynasty, Xin Chenggong and Zhang Daoren in the Song Dynasty, Bao Cai and Zhou Gengyun in the Yuan Dynasty (1206-1368), Dai Jin and Shang Xi in the Ming Dynasty, and Zhang Shanzi, He Xiangning, Jing Zhenchu, Qi Baishi, Liu Jiyou, and Fan Zeng in modern times. The following is a story of the painter Zhang Shanzi and the tiger.

A renowned modern Chinese painter named Zhang Shanzi (1882-1940), a native of Neijiang City, Sichuan Province, was particularly fond of the tiger and a master of tiger painting. He called himself an "adorer of the tiger". To improve his tiger painting techniques, he observed tigers for a long time and even raised tigers himself. The tigers in his works are vivid and powerful, appearing in different postures. Lin Yutang, a famous contemporary Chinese writer, commented on his paintings: "Each and every muscle, backbone, shoulder and claw of the tigers he painted is energetic, dynamic and lifelike."

Zhang Shanzi was a patriotic painter. After the War of Resistance Against Japanese Aggression broke out in China, he held art exhibitions and delivered speeches in France, the United States, and other countries to rally support for China.

He sold his paintings and used the money to fund the anti-Japanese war in China. When he was received by President Franklin D. Roosevelt in 1940, he painted 28 tigers on site, representing the 28 provinces of China at the time. The painting was titled "A Roaring China". As he was told that Claire Lee Chennault would organize the First American Volunteer Group of the Chinese Air Force to assist China in combating Japan, Zhang Shanzi created a painting named "Flying Tigers" for Chennault. The painting of two winged tigers was intended to convey the meaning of the Chinese saying "to be like a tiger with wings", which means "with might redoubled". Chennault liked the painting very much and renamed his group the "Flying Tigers". The Flying Tigers dealt a heavy blow to the Japanese invaders in China, providing meritorious service in the war. In recognition of Chennault's merits, Chinese President Xi Jinping awarded a badge commemorating the 70th anniversary of the victory in the Chinese people's War of Resistance Against Japanese Aggression to Chennault's widow in September 2015. The "Flying Tigers" painting created by Zhang Shanzi is now housed in the Smithsonian Institution.

II. Chinese New Year Paintings

Chinese New Year Paintings are traditional paintings in China that have enjoyed a long history. Most works are characterized by their concise drawing style, bright colors and explicit meanings. This has made them very popular among the Chinese people.

Chinese New Year Paintings throve during the Qing Dynasty, which gave rise to many hubs such as Yangliuqing Town in Tianjin; Yangjiabu Village in Weifang, Shandong Province; Wuqiang County, Hebei Province; Zhuxian Town in Kaifeng, Henan Province; Fengxiang County, Shaanxi Province;

Taohuawu in Suzhou, Jiangsu Province; Mianzhu City, Sichuan Province and Tantou Town in Shaoyang, Hunan Province. Given the different geographical conditions, historical and cultural backgrounds, social customs as well as aesthetic views, Chinese New Year Paintings from various regions often feature different local characteristics.

Chinese New Year Paintings are usually printed and put up during the Spring Festival, which is the most important festival in China every year. The zodiac is always a popular theme.

New Year Woodblock Prints, a traditional printing handicraft, are a specific type of Chinese New Year Paintings. They date back to the Northern Song Dynasty (960-1127) when movable-type printing was invented. Movable-type printing is considered one of the four great inventions in ancient China (i.e., gunpowder, paper, the compass and printing). The woodblock printing procedure goes as follows: The painter draws a picture on a thin piece of paper and places it on a wood board with the image reversed. Then an engraver uses a variety of metal knives to carve the wood according to the picture. The picture's color will determine what type of wood board is needed. If the picture has only one color, one wood board is enough. But if the picture has more than one color, two types of wood boards are needed, namely the ink plate and the color plate. The ink plate is used to print the outline of the picture while the color plate is used to color the picture. The number of color plates is determined by how many colors the picture has. After the ink plates are made, the engraver applies the ink to the ink plate, puts a piece of white paper of a certain size on the plate and presses the paper with a palm fiber brush. The outline of the picture is then printed on the paper. Next, the color plates are carved one by one according to the area of a certain color in the picture and its colors are printed on the paper in the way mentioned above. In this way, wood carving paintings can be mass-produced.

In the eyes of the Chinese people, the tiger is the king of all beasts, so it is one of their favorite zodiac animals. For this reason, there are a lot of tiger-themed Chinese New Year Paintings. Such artwork mainly falls into the following three categories: paintings with the theme of auspiciousness and blessings in the Year of the Tiger; paintings such as door-gods and home-protecting pictures, which show awe-inspiring tigers; paintings of popular folk stories, such as "Wu Song Fights the Tiger" and "The Tiger Learns Skills".

Tiger-themed Sculpture and Ceramics

I. Tiger-themed sculpture

As a large and brightly-colored animal, the tiger looks powerful and majestic. It is quite popular with Chinese people and artists.

As early as the Shang and Zhou dynasties, there was a large number of tiger-shaped bronze ware used as important ritual vessels of the state. A news report in 2018 revealed that a rare Western Zhou piece of bronze ware called *hu ying*, which dates back 3,000 years, was auctioned in Kent, southeast England, at a price of 410,000 pounds. Featuring a tiger-shaped lid and spout, the piece of bronze ware was owned by a former British navy colonel who was among the looters of the Old Summer Palace of China.

In addition, some pieces of tiger-shaped bronze ware for daily use have also been found. The mother-and-son tiger bronze ware, unearthed in Baoji, Shaanxi Province, is an example of exquisite tiger-themed bronze ware of the Western Zhou Dynasty. It has a unique shape — a robust mother tiger holding her cub in her mouth affectionately.

Today, tiger sculptures are mainly seen in public squares. A typical one is the iconic sculpture of the Tiger Beach Ocean Park in Dalian, Liaoning Province. Designed by Han Meilin, a prominent Chinese artist, the tiger sculpture took him two years and nine months to complete. The structure is 35.5 meters long, 6.5 meters high, and weighs over 2,000 tons. It consists of six tigers, which seem to be dashing forward, making a display of overwhelming force.

II. Tiger-themed ceramics

Chinese porcelain has a long history that can be traced back to the Shang Dynasty during the 16th century BC. Along with silk, Chinese porcelain has been a focal point of Chinese culture. After the Tang Dynasty, porcelain wares made during the Song, Yuan, Ming and Qing dynasties established themselves all over the world for their exquisite workmanship and advanced techniques. Porcelain manufacturing techniques have been passed down to modern times. Nowadays, famous porcelain cities and towns, such as Jingdezhen in Jiangxi Province, Dehua in Fujian Province, Yixing in Jiangsu Province, Foshan in Guangdong Province, Zibo in Shandong Province, and Tangshan in Hebei Province are still developing these traditional techniques.

Chinese zodiac porcelain pieces are mostly artifacts and ornaments that are categorized as art porcelain; while some others are for daily use such as the animal ornaments on china tea sets, children's piggy banks, and decoration sets.

Thanks to the unprecedentedly prosperous porcelain industry in the Tang and Song dynasties, there appeared a large number of tiger-themed ceramic products. However, in the Ming and Qing dynasties, tiger-themed porcelain works were rare, and they were mainly impressionistic. In modern times, ceramic works bearing tiger patterns became common again.

The most prestigious contemporary ceramic tiger-painting master was Bi Yuanming (1907-1991) of Jingdezhen, Jiangxi Province. Applying traditional Chinese painting techniques to ceramic fine arts, he formed his own unique artistic style. The tigers in his paintings were vivid and forceful. Hence he was nicknamed "Tiger Bi" by his peers. His representative work is the "Roaring Tiger", a porcelain plate painting used for screen decoration, in which the tiger is majestic and lifelike. From 1959 to 1995, the screen was placed in the Jiangxi Hall of the Great Hall of the People in Beijing. When US President Richard Nixon saw this painting during his visit in China in 1972, he was amazed and expressed to Premier Zhou Enlai his wish to collect its woodblock copy. In 1974, when Chinese leader Deng Xiaoping visited the United States, he presented Nixon with a new porcelain painting of the "Roaring Tiger" re-created by Bi as a token of Sino-US friendship.

Tiger-themed Paper-cuts

Paper-cuts are made by using scissors or knives to cut images or patterns in pieces of paper. Paper-cutting is a Chinese folk art form that often adds flair to both local community activities and everyday life. In China, paper-cutting has a long history and is very popular among the people. It has become an essential part of various folk activities. In May 2006, this traditional form of art was included in the National Intangible Cultural Heritage List. At a meeting held by the United Nations Educational, Scientific and Cultural Organization (UNESCO) in September and October 2009, Chinese paper-cutting was selected as an item in the Representative List of the Intangible Cultural Heritage of Humanity.

The paper-cutting tradition started at the beginning of the Tang Dynasty, became popular in the Song Dynasty and reached its peak during the Ming and Qing dynasties. Paper-cuts fall into the following eight categories based on the patterns that appear on them: figures, birds and other animals, Chinese characters, household utensils and containers, flowers and plants, fruits and vegetables, insects, and landscape. They feature images of praying for blessings, dispelling evil forces, admonishing others and fun living.

Chinese paper-cutting art mainly consists of two schools, the South School and the North School. Foshan, Guangdong Province; Wuhan, Hubei Province; Yangzhou, Jiangsu Province and Zhangpu, Fujian Province are the birthplaces of the South School of Chinese paper-cutting, while the North School is renowned for the pieces produced in Yuxian County, Hebei Province; Gaomi City, Shandong Province; and other localities in Shanxi and Shaanxi provinces. It's worth mentioning that Gaomi is the hometown of Mr. Mo Yan, the 2012 Nobel laureate in Literature.

The Chinese people consider Spring Festival as their most

important festival. Paper-cut window decorations featuring the 12 zodiac animals have been an important way for the people to mark the occasion for generations. Tiger-themed paper-cuts mainly fall into three categories: 1) those for window decoration featuring wishes for and celebration of the Year of the Tiger; 2) large paper-cuts showing awe-inspiring images of tigers, used as door-gods to ward off evils from people's homes. This type of paper-cuts is usually posted on doors or interior walls; 3) paper-cuts created by folk artists based on myths, folklore, operas, literary classics and other stories, such as "Wu Song Fights the Tiger".

Tiger-shaped Tallies and Seals

In the eyes of Chinese people, the tiger is believed to have inviolable majesty and invincible power; therefore, it became a symbol of military power. In ancient China, generals' camps were called "tiger camps"; the military affairs office (equivalent to present-day military command) of the Northern Song Dynasty was called the "White Tiger Hall".

In the Spring and Autumn Period and the Warring States Period, military tokens for troop movements of vassal states were called "Tiger-shaped tallies". Made of gold, silver or copper, the tokens were tiger-shaped. They each had two halves, with the right kept by the monarch or at the court while the left was issued to generals or local officials. Only when the two halves were fitted together could troops be dispatched. In 1973, a tiger-shaped tally of the State of Qin of the Warring States Period was unearthed in a western suburb of Xi'an, Shaanxi Province. This tally, called "Tiger-shaped Tally of Du" (Du is a place name), is the oldest military tally unearthed in China. The inscription on its back reveals the troop mobilization system of the State of Qin. The inscription is embellished with shining gold wire, resembling the patterns on a tiger's coat. It exemplifies the superb gold inlaying techniques that were in use at that time.

During the Han Dynasty, tiger-shaped tallies were made of copper, with inscriptions on the seams. In the Sui and Tang dynasties, tallies resembled other animals. In the Southern Song Dynasty (1127-1279), the tiger shape was re-adopted. In the Yuan Dynasty, the military used tiger-head tallies, which eventually evolved into a variety of military tokens in later generations.

In addition to generals and soldiers who regard tigers as a symbol of bravery and strength, Chinese men of letters also like tiger-themed artwork such as tiger seals. The Chinese literati's tiger seals are rich in content. Some are character-based, featuring the Chinese character for "tiger" in various calligraphic styles or tiger-related aphorisms and idioms. Others show drawings of a tiger.

Tiger-themed Stamps

Zodiac animal stamps are also an important part of Chinese zodiac culture. As China's cultural influence grows, many countries around the world have begun issuing zodiac animal stamps during the Spring Festival.

After the founding of the People's Republic of China in 1949, China Post issued stamps featuring the Siberian Tiger and the South China Tiger to protect the endangered tiger species. Released on July 20, 1979, the Siberian-Tiger-themed stamps were based on the Chinese paintings of Siberian Tigers by the prominent Chinese painter Liu Jiyou. Each set consisted of three different stamps, namely, *Roar*, *Intimacy*, and *Taking a Rest*, which had a face value of 4 *fen*, 8 *fen*, and 60 *fen* respectively. The South-China-Tiger-themed stamps, released on August 23, 2004, were designed mainly by animal painter Liu Jibiao. It was a set of two: one featured a head of a South China tiger and was worth 80 *fen*; the other was titled *Mother and Babies*, showing a tigress lying on a gravel ground with one cub on her back and the other to her front. It had a value of two yuan.

In 1980, China Post began to issue Chinese zodiac animal stamps. The first was the Zodiac Monkey stamp, and in 1986 the first Zodiac Tiger stamp was released. The tiger image on the stamp looked like a cloth toy tiger and also had the style of a paper-cut. It had a value of 8 *fen*. However, its current market price is 50 yuan, reflecting its value for collectors. By

2018, China Post had issued a total of three kinds of Zodiac Tiger stamps: the 1986 version, the 1998 version, and the 2010 version.

During the Spring Festival, post offices across China also offer zodiac animal postmarks, which are mainly composed of zodiac animal images with some characters. They are stamped on letters or commemorative postal products.

Zodiac tiger stamp in 1986

Zodiac tiger stamp in 2010

第四章 关于虎的中国本土艺术表现形式

一、关于虎的中国绘画艺术

1. 国画

中国传统的绘画形式是用毛笔蘸水、墨、彩作画于绢或纸上，简称“国画”。其主要题材分人物、山水、花鸟等。

12 生肖题材的绘画在中国自古至今都是一个重要的绘画题材。每当虎年到来时，生肖虎就会成为中国画家当年绘画作品的主角。

中国人自远古时代就很崇拜虎，在许多大山的岩壁上都发现有虎岩画，在一些出土的汉代墓葬中也发现很多精美的虎画像。历史上有许多以画虎闻名的中国画家，如：唐代的李渐，宋代的辛成工、张道人，元代的包采、周耕云，明代的戴进、尚喜，以及近现代的张善子、何香凝、荆振初、齐白石、刘继卣、范曾等人。下面我们就介绍一下画家张善子与老虎的故事。

张善子(1882—1940)是中国近代著名画虎大师，四川省内江人。他绘画功底深厚，极其喜欢虎，擅于画虎，还自称为“虎痴”。他为了画好虎，自己饲养老虎，以便于长期观察虎。他笔下的老虎形象逼真，姿态各异，威武苍劲，可谓形神兼备。与他同时代的中国著名作家林语堂这样评价他的画作：“他画的老虎，凡一肌、一脊、一肩、一爪，无不精力磅礴，精纯逼真。”

张善子是一位爱国画家。中国抗日战争爆发后，他在法国、美国等地举办画展、演讲宣传抗日救国，出售自己的画作筹集款项支援抗日斗争。1940 年，他在受到美国罗斯福总统接见时当场画下 28 只猛虎，代表当时中国的 28 个省份，画作以“中国怒吼了”为题。当他得知美国人陈纳德要组建美国志愿援华航空队进行抗日作战，张善子特意创作一幅《飞虎图》送给陈纳德将军。《飞虎图》借中国典故“如虎添翼”的寓意，画了两只长着翅膀的老虎。陈纳德非常喜欢，还将航空志愿队改名为“飞虎队”。飞虎队在中国境内沉重打击了日军，立下赫赫战功。2015 年 9 月，中国国家主席习近平向陈纳德遗孀颁发了抗战胜利 70 周年纪念章，以表彰其功勋。张善子创作的《飞虎图》现藏于美国国家博物馆。

2. 中国年画

中国年画是拥有悠久历史的一种传统绘画形式，其特点是绘制简单，色彩鲜艳，寓意直白，深受百姓喜爱，在民间流传非常广泛。

中国年画在清代高度繁荣，逐渐形成一些年画集散地，如天津的杨柳青镇、山东潍坊的杨家埠村、河北的武强县、河南开封的朱仙镇、陕西的凤翔县、江苏苏州的桃花坞、四川的绵竹，以及湖南邵阳的滩头镇，等等。不同地区的年画因地理环境、历史文化、世俗风尚、审美趣味的不同而呈现出鲜明的地方特色。

中国年画往往在中国人一年中最重要的节日——春节时印制并张贴，每一年的主题少不了生肖年画。因此，12 生肖成为中国年画重要且不可缺少的创作主题。

木版年画是中国年画中一种古老的手工印刷传统工艺，其根源可以追溯到中国古代的四大发明之一——北宋时期发明的活字印刷术。具体制作方法是：画师先在薄纸上绘制图画，然后将薄纸反贴在木板上，由刻工使用各种金属刀具在木板上雕刻成形。刻工需要根据画师绘制的图画是单色还是多色来雕刻木版：如果是单色画就只需雕刻一块木版；如果是多种颜色画就需要雕刻两种木版。单色画只有一块木版，用于印制图画的线条轮廓，一般使用黑色油墨，所以称作“墨版”。多种颜色画除雕刻一块墨版外，还要雕刻“色版”，根据图画颜色多少决定刻制多少块色版。墨版和色版刻好后，印工们就可以在刻工雕刻好的墨版上涂上油墨，然后将已裁剪好固定尺寸的白纸放置在墨版上，用棕毛刷按压白纸，木板上雕刻的图案线条轮廓就印在了白纸上。然后继续按照这样的做法，使用不同色版给年画的空白部分添加红、黄、蓝等颜色。如此就可以批量印制同一图案的彩色年画了。

因为老虎是中国人心目中的“百兽之王”，是中国人最喜爱的生肖动物之一，所以关于虎的年画作品特别丰富。关于虎的年画作品主要分为三大类：第一类是虎年以吉祥、祈福为主题的年画；第二类是借助虎威而创作的门神图、镇宅图等年画；第三类则是流传度较高的民间故事年画，例如《武松打虎》《老虎学艺》等。

二、关于虎的雕塑和陶瓷作品

1. 关于虎的雕塑作品

由于老虎体型高大、毛色斑斓，极具力量和威严，所以深受中国大众和艺术创作者的青睐。

中国商周时期就有大量虎形的青铜器作为国家重要的祭祀礼器。2018 年有报道称，距今约 3000 年的稀有西周青铜器“虎蓥（yíng）”在英国东南部肯特郡拍卖，最终以 41 万英镑成交。这个青铜器因其器盖和出水口的老虎造型而得名。它由一位曾经参与了火烧圆明园的英国海军上校拥有。

此外，还有一些用于生活的虎形青铜器。出土于陕西宝鸡的西周时期青铜器母子虎是这个时期虎主题青铜器的精品之作。该青铜器造型独具匠心，一只健壮的母虎口衔一只小老虎，表现了舐犊情深之意。

今天，老虎的雕塑多见于广场。比较有代表性的是大连老虎滩海洋公园的标志性雕塑——虎雕。这座虎雕由中国著名美术家韩美林设计制作，耗时两年九个月。虎雕长35.5米，高6.5米，重2000多吨。虎雕由六只老虎组成，呈奔腾向前状，气势逼人。

2. 关于虎的陶瓷作品

中国陶瓷制作历史悠久，可以追溯到公元前16世纪的商代。中国陶瓷曾经一度与丝绸一起成为中国文化的代名词。尤其是唐朝以后，宋、元、明、清代的瓷器以精美绝伦著称于世。陶瓷制作延续至今，逐渐形成了江西景德镇、福建德化、江苏宜兴、广东佛山、山东淄博、河北唐山等多个当代中国知名的“陶瓷之城”。

12 生肖的陶瓷作品大多为艺术摆件和玩物，应该属于艺术陶瓷范畴。但也有部分作品具有日用陶瓷的功能，如茶具上的陶瓷宠物、陶瓷储钱罐以及陶瓷摆件等。

唐宋时期由于陶瓷业空前繁盛，所以虎主题的陶瓷作品较多。明清两代瓷器的虎作品不多见，且多为写意之作。到了近代，以虎为纹饰的陶瓷作品又变得较为常见。

在当代最负盛名的陶瓷虎绘工艺大师是江西景德镇的陶瓷美术家毕渊明（1907–1991）。毕渊明将中国传统画技法应用于陶瓷美术，所画之虎形神兼备，威猛霸气，形成了自己独特的艺术风格，被同行们敬送绰号“毕老虎”。毕渊明的代表作品是屏风瓷板画《虎啸图》，图中老虎八面威风，呼之欲出。该屏风曾于 1959—1995 年摆放于北京人民大会堂江西厅。1972 年，时任美国总统尼克松访华时看到这幅《虎啸图》惊叹不已，向周恩来总理表达了想收藏一块《虎啸图》版画的愿望。1974 年，中国领导人邓小平访美时，携带毕渊明重新创作的一块《虎啸图》瓷板赠送给了尼克松，作为中美友谊的信物。

三、关于虎的剪纸

中国剪纸是用剪刀或刻刀在纸上剪刻花纹或图形，用于装点生活或配合其他民俗活动的一种民间艺术。在中国，剪纸具有悠久历史和广泛的群众基础，是各种民俗活动的重要组成部分。2006年5月，剪纸艺术被列入中国第一批国家级非物质文化遗产名录。2009年9—10月，在联合国教科文组织保护非物质文化遗产政府间委员会第四次会议上，中国剪纸项目入选“人类非物质文化遗产代表作名录”。

中国剪纸的流行始于唐朝初期，宋代在民间普及，明清两代空前兴盛。中国剪纸根据纹样图案可以大致分为人物、鸟兽、文字、器皿、花木、果蔬、昆虫、山水等八类，主要表现纳吉祝福、驱邪除恶、劝勉警戒、生活趣味等主题。

中国剪纸流派主要分南、北两派：南派剪纸发祥地主要有广东佛山、湖北武汉、江苏扬州、福建漳浦等地；北派剪纸以河北蔚县、山东高密、山西和陕西等地剪纸最为出名。山东高密是中国第一位获得诺贝尔文学奖者——莫言先生的家乡。

春节是中国人最重视的节日。因此，用于春节的12生肖窗花剪纸是中国人世代相传、永恒不变的主题。老虎题材的剪纸主要分为三类：一是生肖虎年祈福、欢庆节日的窗花剪纸；二是借助虎的神威，用作门神、镇宅之用的幅面较大的剪纸，一般张贴在门扇或室内墙壁之上；三是民间艺人的主题性创作剪纸，主要表现的是神话传说、民间故事、戏曲故事及文学名著中的经典片段等，例如“武松打虎”等。

四、军队虎符令牌与文人虎形印章

在中国人心目之中，虎具有不可侵犯的威严和不可战胜的力量。因此，虎成为军权的象征。在古代中国，军队将帅的帐篷被称为“虎帐”，军机处理要地（相当于今天的军队司令部）被称为“白虎堂”，等等。

春秋战国时期，各个诸侯国的调兵令牌被称为“虎符”。虎符是指铸刻成老虎形状的兵符，可用金、银、铜等材质。虎符分为左右两半，右半存于国君或朝廷，左半由统兵将领或地方官持有，只有两半兵符合二为一才能调动军队。1973年，从西安西郊出土的一枚战国时期秦国的虎符——杜虎符（杜为地名），成为中国出土年代最早的兵符。该虎符背面上刻有铭文，说明了当时秦国的调兵制度。铭文上嵌有金丝，金光闪亮，远望极像虎皮斑纹，体现了高超的错金工艺水平。

到了汉朝，虎符均为铜质，骑缝刻有铭文，以右半为尊。隋唐时代改用其他动物形状作为兵符。南宋时期恢复使用虎符，元代改用虎头令牌，最终演变为后世的各式调兵令牌。

军队将士喜欢老虎，将其视为勇猛和力量的象征。中国文人也喜欢刻制虎形印章。中国文人的虎印章内容非常丰富，有的展示“虎”的各种书法字体或与虎相关的警句、成语等，有的通过线条表现虎的各种形态。

五、关于生肖虎的邮票

生肖邮票也是中国生肖文化体现的一个重要领域，而且随着中国文化影响力的扩大，世界上很多国家在中国春节期间也发行生肖邮票。

1949 年新中国成立后，为了保护濒临灭绝的老虎物种，中国邮政先后发行了“东北虎”和“华南虎”特种邮票。“东北虎”邮票发行于 1979 年 7 月 20 日，图案取自著名画家刘继卣关于东北虎的中国画，一套 3 枚，分别为 4 分面值的“咆哮”、8 分面值的“相依”和 60 分面值的“休憩”。“华南虎”邮票发行于 2004 年 8 月 23 日，主要设计者为动物画家刘继彪，一套两枚，一枚面值 80 分，票面是一只华南虎的头部特写，另一枚面值 2 元，名为“母子情”，画面为卧在碎石地上的母虎背上驮着一只小虎，另有一只小虎卧在母虎前面的地上。

1980 年中国邮政开始发行中国生肖邮票，第一枚是生肖猴票，1986 年诞生了第一枚生肖虎邮票。画面采用民间装饰手法，既具有布玩具虎的韵味，又有剪纸的格调，且不失真虎的本质。这枚虎年邮票当时发行面值为 8 分人民币，现在市场价格为 50 元人民币，具有一定的收藏价值。截至 2018 年，中国邮政一共发行了 3 枚生肖虎邮票：1986 年虎票、1998 年虎票和 2010 年虎票。

中国各地邮局在春节前后还会推出生肖邮戳，形式多采用生肖动物形象加一点文字构成，在信件或纪念邮品上加盖。

Appendix:

Table of Chinese Zodiac Animals and Their Corresponding Christian Years (1912-2031)

shǔ
鼠

1912 1972
1924 1984
1936 1996
1948 2008
1960 2020

niú
牛

1913 1973
1925 1985
1937 1997
1949 2009
1961 2021

hǔ
虎

1914 1974
1926 1986
1938 1998
1950 2010
1962 2022

tù
兔

1915 1975
1927 1987
1939 1999
1951 2011
1963 2023

lóng
龙

1916 1976
1928 1988
1940 2000
1952 2012
1964 2024

shé
蛇

1917 1977
1929 1989
1941 2001
1953 2013
1965 2025

mǎ
马

1918 1978
1930 1990
1942 2002
1954 2014
1966 2026

yáng
羊

1919 1979
1931 1991
1943 2003
1955 2015
1967 2027

hóu
猴

1920 1980
1932 1992
1944 2004
1956 2016
1968 2028

jī
鸡

1921 1981
1933 1993
1945 2005
1957 2017
1969 2029

gǒu
狗

1922 1982
1934 1994
1946 2006
1958 2018
1970 2030

zhū
猪

1923 1983
1935 1995
1947 2007
1959 2019
1971 2031

责任编辑：翟淑蓉
英文编辑：吴爱俊
英文审定：卢　敏 James Hutchison
封面设计：厚　冬
责任印制：汪　洋

图书在版编目（CIP）数据

生肖虎 : 英、汉 / 张立章编著. -- 北京 : 华语教学出版社, 2018.12
(中国生肖文化解读系列)
ISBN 978-7-5138-1642-7

Ⅰ. ①生… Ⅱ. ①张… Ⅲ. ①汉语—对外汉语教学—语言读物 ②十二生肖—文化
Ⅳ. ①H195.5②K892.21

中国版本图书馆CIP数据核字(2018)第241030号

本书获得北方工业大学出版基金的资助，在此表示感谢。

中国生肖文化解读系列·生肖虎

张立章 编著

华语教学出版社有限责任公司出版
(中国北京百万庄大街24号 邮政编码 100037)
电话: (86)10-68320585 68997826
传真: (86)10-68997826 68326333
网址: www.sinolingua.com.cn
电子信箱: hyjx@sinolingua.com.cn
北京玺诚印务有限公司印刷
2019 年（32 开）第1 版
2019 年第1 版第1 次印刷
(英汉)
ISBN 978-7-5138-1642-7
定价: 49.00元